juggling
1-2-3

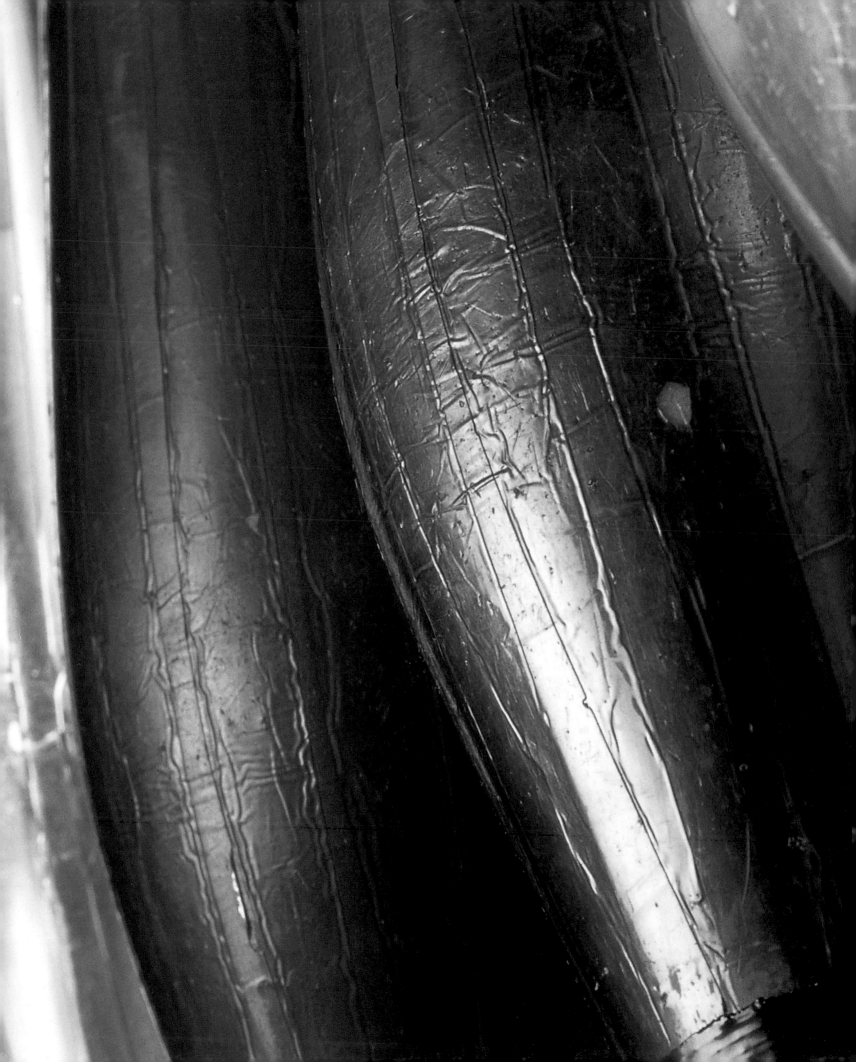

juggling 1-2-3

Henrik Lind

Sterling Publishing Co., Inc.
New York

Creative director: Sarah King
Editor: Clare Haworth-Maden
Project editor: Judith Millidge
Designer: Axis Design

Library of Congress Cataloging-in-Publication Data Available

10   9   8   7   6   5   4   3   2   1

Published in 2003 by Sterling Publishing Co. Inc.
387 Park Avenue South
New York, N.Y. 10016

First published in 2001 under the title Master Juggling
by D&S Books Ltd
Kerswell, Parkham Ash
Bideford, Devon, EX39 5PR

Distributed in Canada by Sterling Publishing
c/o Canadian Manda Group,
One Atlantic Avenue, Suite 105
Toronto, Ontario, Canada M6K 3E7, Canada

Every effort has been made to ensure that all the information in this book is accurate.
however, due to differing conditions, tools, and individual skills, the publisher cannot
be responsible for any injuries, losses, and other damages which may result from the
use of the information in this book.

Printed in Singapore

214751

Sterling ISBN 1-4027-0877-7

Contents

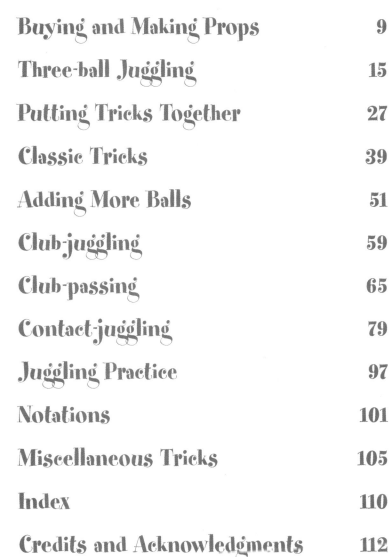

Introduction

Juggling is Not Interesting!

Well, not interesting enough to make it into the history books, anyway. Of course, there is some information to be found if you're really intrigued. Hieroglyphics and stone carvings from ancient Egypt show people juggling, and the Romans also knew about it. One legend mentions a legionnaire who used to juggle to amuse the troops. Jesters in medieval Europe certainly juggled, but there is no record of how good they were or which juggling patterns they used. Many stories tell us that they were capable of superhuman feats, but it is impossible to prove these tales now.

Modern juggling, from the early years of the twentieth century, is naturally much better documented. Some of these jugglers were capable of seemingly impossible tricks, and the records are rather more reliable sources than legends and stone carvings. Paul Cinquevalli, Enrico Rastelli, and Francis Brunn were the best jugglers of their day, not just in advanced juggling, but in demonstrating equilibrium at its highest level. They performed ball-balancing, bouncing, spinning, multiple ring, and club juggling acts that many other jugglers tried in vain to copy. Most importantly, their juggling acts were actually recorded in some way, in writing, drawing, or on film. If you're interested in how it was done in the good old days, the internet is a good place to begin your research.

But this is neither a history lesson, nor a book about how juggling looked in the early days. The sole purpose of this book is actually to teach you how to juggle, not just the basics, but the more advanced stuff as well.

Learning how to juggle is not that hard, especially if you have a teacher, a really good juggler with lots of time on his or her hands. Learning to juggle by reading a book is completely different: you'll have a brief explanation, some tips, and off you go. No one is there to correct you, no one tells you how you are doing. You don't have anyone to share ideas, success, and failure with, and finally, your learning progress will probably take more time.

This is called the hard way and was how I learned to juggle. The first struggling steps of the three-ball cascade took place in my own kitchen many years ago.

Jugglers are social creatures, they like to be seen, to show off, and to exchange ideas with other jugglers. Regular workshops take place virtually everywhere, and if you find a juggling group that practices together on a regular basis, you have struck gold. Hang on to them, because you could learn a a great deal from them.

These people are light years away from the traditional circus jugglers (the ones wearing tight Lycra costumes, with lightning-fast routines, perfect teeth, and silly names). Social jugglers are more likely to be students or high-school-drop-out hippie-wannabees. Many jugglers are vegetarian and vegetarian dishes are always the main course at the big juggling conventions around the world. But absolutely anyone can take up juggling.

Juggling is actually good for you. It sharpens your reflexes and reactions, and exercises your mental faculties. Trying to solve a complex juggling riddle keeps you on the competitive edge. Special juggling workshops are available for business people that help them to become less stressed and more focused. Some juggling books introduce Zen and lateral thinking into the juggling. I totally agree; I still juggle a simple cascade when I want to chill out; looking at the infinity sign of the dancing balls really calms the nerves, and the feeling of success after untangling a complex pattern is unbeatable.

So what is juggling then? One common definition is "to throw things around in the air." This is not bad, but how many "things"? One ball? Two balls? More balls than hands? What about contact juggling, where you roll balls on your body? Is this also juggling? Balancing a burning torch on your nose? Or how about spinning a credit card on your middle finger? There are probably as many definitions as there are jugglers. My own definition is quite simple. If you're doing something wonderful and complex with balls, clubs, or something, and you're hanging around with other crazy people like yourself, you're probably a juggler.

7

On With the Show!

Props

Buying and Making Props

Buying juggling props can be frustrating. Walk into any juggling store, and the chances are that you'll be faced with a bewildering array of balls of every type of material, shape, color, and size, along with big clubs, small clubs, clubs with short and long handles, and fast— or slow—spinning clubs. This chapter will help you to decide which props you need, as well as how many.

Buy balls in light colors when you begin. Balls of different colors will help you keep track during tricky moves.

Transparent balls look stunning when contact-juggling, but they are expensive and easily damaged, so take good care of them.

Beanbag balls are best for the beginner as they don't roll too far when dropped.

White silicon balls are the first choice of all serious jugglers. They may be expensive, but you will soon be hooked!

Choosing Your Juggling Balls

When you begin juggling, you'll need at least four balls: three to practice with and a spare. It's a good idea to buy balls that are light in color, like white or bright yellow; although black balls may look stylish, they are harder to juggle with because they're difficult to see. It's also advisable to buy one differently colored ball to enable you to see which ball is going where when you're practicing a really tricky move.

The best balls for beginners are beanbags, heavy balls that make a satisfying thud when they're dropped and don't have the annoying habit of bouncing or rolling under the sofa when they hit the ground.

When you've mastered juggling with beanbags, the next balls to buy are stage balls, which hardly bounce at all. Stage balls are made of plastic and are available in a wide variety of

The Beginner's Shopping List

4 light-colored beanbags

(including 1 spare)

1 different-colored beanbag

5 stage balls

1 large stage ball

4 small acrylic balls

1 large acrylic ball

4 pool balls

3 white silicone balls

10 clubs (7 matching, 3 spare)

It is better to spend money on good-quality clubs. Not only do they handle well, they look great!

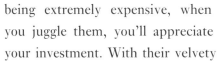

different sizes. If you're practicing solo contact-juggling, a large stage ball is ideal.

Transparent acrylic balls are the contact-juggler's choice. Although they are mesmerizing to watch, they're very expensive and scratch easily, so separate them from each other when storing them to avoid them scratching each other. If you're practicing multiple-ball work, such as palm-spinning, buy a set of pool balls, which, despite being made of the same material, are less expensive than acrylic balls.

Bouncing balls are excellent if you tend to miss your catches, as they simply bounce back. Available in a range of materials and at different prices, the cheapest ones are usually adequate if you're planning to work on some bouncing tricks.

However, for more serious bouncers and, of course, the three-ball purist, there is really only one choice: silicone balls. Despite being extremely expensive, when you juggle them, you'll appreciate your investment. With their velvety surface, perfect spherical shape, and rebound to die for, you'll be hooked for life. White is the professional juggler's color of choice when buying silicone balls.

Choosing Your Clubs

Although many jugglers advocate buying seven clubs, I recommend that you always buy ten so that you have a replacement at hand if you break or lose a club. Ideally, buy seven matching clubs and the remaining three in different colors, either to practice with or for three-club routines.

Buy expensive, good-quality clubs. You won't regret it: cheap clubs look dull, have unpleasantly soft handles and an unbalanced weight, and are derided by professional jugglers. It is important that you test-juggle clubs before buying them. If they tend to smack you in the face, have rock-hard handles, or a hammerlike spin, don't buy them. Try out as many clubs as you can and buy the ones that feel right for you. Because clubs are bigger than balls, they don't have to be white in order for you to see them, so choose whichever color catches your eye.

Some jugglers prefer to make their own props rather than buying them. If, like them, you consider the props that are sold in juggling stores to be prohibitively expensive, here's how to make a beanbag, torches, and clubs.

11

Making Your Own Props

A Beanbag

A beanbag is one of the easiest props to make. Choose any fabric you like—some jugglers make excellent beanbags from old jeans—but for a deluxe beanbag I'd recommend suede or synthetic leather. The color is up to you, but make sure that the beanbag's size suits your hands.

1 Either photocopy the pattern or trace over it using a pencil and a piece of tracing paper. Cut out the copied pattern and pin it to the fabric. Now cut out the fabric shape. You will need four segments of fabric to make one ball, so cut out three more fabric shapes.

2 Take two segments and place them together, right sides facing each other. Using either a needle and thread or a sewing machine, stitch one side together. Repeat for the two remaining segments.

3 Take the paired segments and, with the right sides on the inside, place them together so that they resemble balls. Stitch the paired segments together, leaving a small section open. Turn the ball inside out through the open section.

4 Fill the ball with rice or couscous and then sew up the hole.

You Will Need

tracing paper (optional)

pencil (optional)

scissors

pins

fabric

needle*

thread

packet of rice or couscous

* or a sewing machine, particularly if you're making a lot of beanbags

12

Three Torches

Not only do home-made torches often spin as well as the real thing, but they look good and are cheap and easy to make. You'll probably find an inexpensive chair in a second-hand furniture store. Club knobs are sold by juggling stores, and it's best to buy them first so that you can check that they fit the chair before you buy it. When choosing your chair, also look at the legs and ask yourself if they look jugglable. They should ideally be round, rather than square, and quite narrow at the ends.

1 Using a saw, cut the legs from the chair. Now try juggling three of the legs to see how they feel. If necessary, adjust the length or balance by sawing off small sections.

2 Attach a club knob to the narrow end of each of the three chair legs in turn.

3 Using scissors, cut the buckles off the belts. Now attach each belt to the other end of each chair leg using a screwdriver, screws, and washers.

Three Clubs

Although home-made clubs are tricky to make, they can be useful substitutes for the real thing. Before investing in their expensive professional counterparts, try juggling these clubs for a while to find out if you're a club-juggler or not. They may look cheap, but they are actually fine to juggle with.

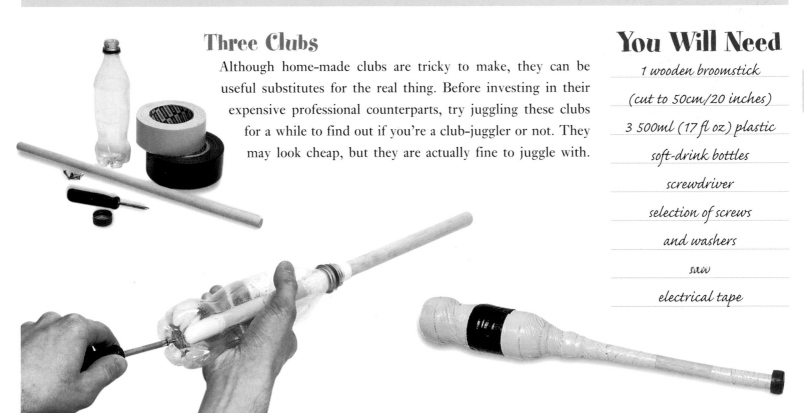

1 Insert the broomstick into the first bottle so that it touches the bottom. Using a screwdriver, secure the broomstick to the bottle with a screw and washer. Repeat for the remaining two bottles.

2 Now wrap the electrical tape around each bottle in turn until they are completely covered. The tape is the key to the correct balance and feel of the club and the more tape you use, the heavier the club. But beware: the tape also affects the spin, and the hard part is making all three clubs equal in weight.

13

Three-ball Juggling

Learning the Three-ball Cascade

Not only is the three-ball cascade one of the purest of juggling patterns, it is also a starting point and a pattern that you can fall back on when you're finding a new one impossible to master. This pattern resembles the symbol of infinity and will go on and on—just like your own development once you're hooked on juggling. It should be practiced until it's as liquid as water, as polished as marble, and as smooth as velvet.

16

Learning the pattern is easy (you'll probably master the basics in an afternoon or two), and is simply a matter of both of your hands taking turns in throwing and catching three balls, one ball at a time. Unless you're an experienced juggler, your brain will probably not be used to calculating the flight paths of three different objects at once, however, so when learning the pattern, it's best to break it down into steps.

The Three-ball Cascade: Step 1

The first step is to familiarize yourself with the basic throw by practicing throwing one ball back and forth, from one hand to the other.

The three-ball cascade is the starting point for all jugglers, and is one of the purest patterns.

1 Hold the ball in your right hand and then, using a scooping motion, aim it toward your left hand, releasing the ball when it is in front of your stomach. The ball should rise in a pleasing arc to about head height and then fall downward, enabling your left hand to catch it comfortably.

2 Now practice making the same throw without looking at your hands. In order for your brain to calculate the ball's flight path, you'll need to glimpse it when it's at its highest point, however. Perform fifty throws each way.

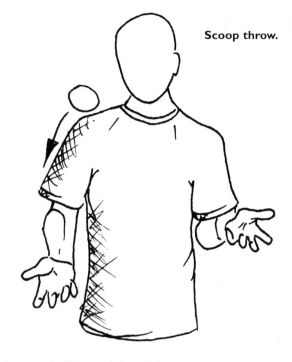

Scoop throw.

The Three-ball Cascade: Step 2

The next step is the most important. It's quite tricky, so don't be too hard on yourself if you don't succeed the first twenty or so times that you try it. It will take your brain quite a few minutes to come to terms with it, but once you have learned this new skill, you're halfway there.

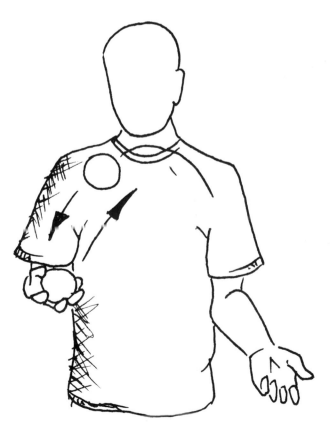

1 Take one ball in each hand, but, rather than throwing them, visualize the following exchange. Throw the ball in your right hand toward your left, clearing your left hand for the catch when the ball is at the peak of its flight by throwing the second ball so that it passes underneath the first one. A split second after the second throw, your left hand should catch the first ball, your right hand then catching the second ball.

2 Now try it for real. Don't worry if you find it difficult—this means that your brain is working hard to solve the problem—it will become easier the more you practice. The following tips may help.

3 Don't follow the balls with your eyes. Only look at them when they are at the peak of their flight.

4 When you have made fifty throws one way, practice the exchange the other way around, starting with your left hand instead of your right. To make the exchange easier, try counting out loud when you're throwing. For example, on the first throw, you could say "One," and on the second, "Two." Alternatively, you could say "Throw," "Throw." It may sound silly, but you'll find that this helps.

5 Another tip that may help if you're really stuck is not to catch the balls at all. Instead, throw them and then let them drop to the ground, first the right-hand ball and then the left underneath it.

17

The Three-ball Cascade: Step 3

When you feel that you've mastered the exchange both ways round, try piecing the steps together to form the full three-ball cascade.

1 Pick up three balls, two in your right hand and one in your left.

2 Try to perform three throws and three catches, as follows. Pass one of the balls in your right hand to the left, using a relaxed, scooping motion. Release the ball when your hand moves in front of your stomach and glance at it when it has risen to about head height. As this ball starts to descend, throw the ball in your left hand underneath it in the same way as before, catching the first ball in your left hand a split second later. When the second ball is about to land in your right hand, throw the last ball from your right hand underneath the descending ball and then catch the second ball. Glance at the third ball as it peaks before heading for your left hand, where it should come safely to rest.

You probably didn't master the three-ball cascade the first time you tried, but keep visualizing what it should look like and carry on practicing. The key is step 2, the exchange, when as soon as a ball starts to descend toward an already occupied hand, the hand clears itself by throwing its ball underneath the descending ball. The three-ball cascade is simply an extended sequence of exchanges.

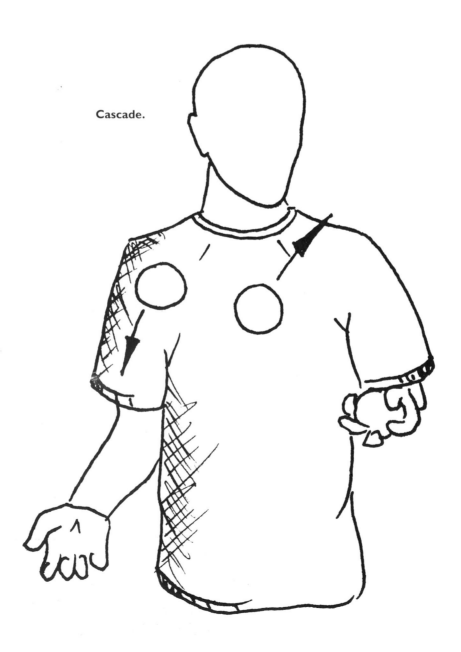

Cascade.

Troubleshooting

Q. I can't perform the exchange. Am I doing something wrong?

A. The problem may either be that you have practiced too much and have become tired and frustrated, causing you to forget the basics, or that you have become impatient to move on to the next step and haven't practiced the exchange enough. In the first instance, have a rest, perhaps do something else, and only try again when you feel refreshed. Always try to stop practicing before feelings of frustration overwhelm you. In the second instance, don't push yourself: take it easy, and everything will suddenly fall into place. Learning should be fun, especially learning how to juggle.

You will find that you often drop balls when you begin —but do persevere.

Q. I'm finding it impossible to throw the third ball. It either sticks to my hand or hurtles away from me at a dangerously high speed. What should I do?

A. The key is to relax. Try performing the three throws without catching the balls, saying "One, two, three" out loud as you throw the balls and then letting each fall to the floor. Now repeat the process, this time catching only the first ball. When you've mastered this, practice catching the first two balls of the sequence before moving on to the full three-ball cascade.

Q. The pattern seems to have a life of its own and is threatening to run away from me. Can you give me any tips?

A. It seems to be in the nature of the freedom-loving cascade to try to run away from its creator. In order to hold onto it, simply practice it while facing a wall. Although you'll probably end up with scratched knuckles, you'll tame it in no time.

20

Q. I've mastered the first few throws. In fact, I can perform ten throws, but no more. Do you have any idea why not?

A. Well done! Performing ten throws is a major feat. Keep practicing, and you'll find that the cascade will become more pure and fluid every day. The space that it occupies will decrease, while its velocity and the number of catches that it incorporates will increase.

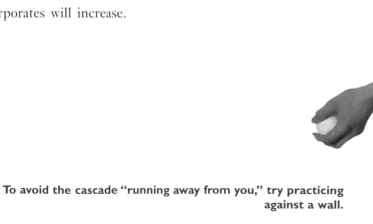

To avoid the cascade "running away from you," try practicing against a wall.

Beyond the Cascade

If you've been practicing the three-ball cascade, you're probably finding juggling less of an effort. You may also be becoming bored and hungry for a new challenge, however. This is a useful stage to learn a few tricks that will give your juggling skills a stable foundation. Some of them are quite easy to learn, but others will take some time. And while some are harder than the three-ball cascade, others are simply distortions of the shapes that appear in the cascade.

Over the Top

"Over the top" is an apt name for this trick, in which one ball is thrown over the top of the cascade.

1 Start to juggle a really relaxed cascade. Look at the pattern and imagine that every peaking ball is a mountain top.

21

2 Without changing your rhythm or throwing order, throw one ball outside of the pattern so that it travels over the top of the "mountains." This is a real mind-over-muscle exercise, and you will have to prepare yourself mentally to make your throwing hand perform this awkward new manouver. Using a different-colored ball may help.

Over the top.

Under the Hand

After you've learned the under-the-hand trick, you can combine it with the over-the-top trick to give you an array of juggling possibilities. It may take some time before you can perform the trick effortlessly, but once learned, it will never be forgotten.

Under the hand.

1 Start juggling another relaxed cascade, but this time watch your hands rather than the pattern, particularly the small, "U"-shaped, scooping motion that every hand makes just before it releases the ball. The scooping motion is the key to the trick: you need to extend the motion so that it passes under your other hand. It may help to practice it without using balls.

2 When you're clear about what to do, start to juggle with three balls, one of which should be a different color to the other two. When this ball lands in your right hand, extend the scooping motion so that you throw it under the other hand more or less vertically before catching it. In other words, although the ball travels from your right to your left hand as usual, it takes a different route.

23

Two in One Hand

The two-in-one-hand trick is probably the most important trick for both beginner and more advanced three-ball juggler alike. The name speaks for itself: you simply juggle two balls in one hand in one of three different ways: rolling out, rolling in, and columns.

A common mistake that many people make when learning the two-in-one-hand trick is juggling the balls toward themselves, or breaking what jugglers call the "wall plane." For example, because no balls are thrown either toward or out from your body, the three-ball cascade stays within the wall plane. To clarify the concept further, if you threw a ball to someone else, you'd be breaking the wall plane.

Two in one hand is an important trick for beginners and experienced jugglers alike.

24

Rolling Out

In the rolling-out pattern, your hand throws on the inside and catches on the outside. A good way to learn this is to start juggling a three-ball cascade and then to go into the two-in-one-hand pattern for a couple of throws. When you start to lose control, simply return to the cascade. You'll only manage a couple of throws at first, but will soon get the hang of it.

Although it's very tempting to juggle the two-in-one-hand pattern using your dominant hand, don't neglect your weaker hand. It's far better to start practicing with your weaker hand and then to transfer to your stronger hand. In fact, you may be amazed to find that your dominant hand has learned the pattern without you being aware of it.

Rolling In

Rolling in is the mirror image of rolling out: the balls are caught on the inside and thrown on the outside. It's neither a common nor a useful juggling manouver, however.

Columns

When juggling two in one hand in columns, the balls rise and fall side by side, just like two elevators in a building. It's one of the most useful tricks there are, and a number of three-ball tricks are based on it. There are many ways to learn this useful pattern. This is one; see also "one up, two up" on page 29.

Holding two balls in your right hand and one in your left, visualize three columns in front of you. Starting in column one, the right-hand column, juggle the balls as follows.

1 Throw the first ball in your right hand straight upward within the right-hand column.

2 Throw the second ball in your right hand straight upward within the middle column and then quickly pull your hand back to catch the first ball.

3 Throw the ball in your left hand into the left-hand column and then catch the ball in the middle column.

4 Using your left hand, throw up the ball that you've just caught into the middle column and then bring your left hand back to the left-hand column to catch the first ball that it threw.

5 So the pattern continues, the balls being thrown in a right, middle, left, middle, right sequence, and the order in which you use your hands being right, right, left, left.

Putting Tricks Together

Putting Together the Basic Tricks

By now you should be able to juggle a cascade effortlessly and should have practiced the fundamental tricks a few times, preferably using both of your hands. Now it's time to start putting them together.

You may already have noticed that if you carry on juggling one of the basic tricks continuously on one side of the pattern, it will form a new pattern. Juggling a trick using the same ball will also form another pattern. Four ways of discovering new tricks or patterns are as follows.

- Juggle the trick using any ball at random.
- Practice the trick using the same ball every time.
- Juggle the trick continuously, using the same hand.
- And finally, juggle every ball using both hands continuously!

To illustrate these methods, let's see how the over-the-top trick—which is already an example of using any ball at random, in that a ball flies over the basic three-ball cascade every now and then—can be evolved. If you send the same ball over the top every time, your pattern will be transformed into something that resembles a game of tennis, with one ball bobbing back and forth over the rest. If you juggle the trick using every right-hand throw to send a ball over the top while your left hand carries on as normal, the balls will follow each other in a loop. Finally, the hardest method of juggling the trick is to juggle every ball with both hands every time. In this case, the resulting trick is called a "reverse cascade."

Another way of creating a new pattern is to combine two tricks. To create a windmill, for example, simply throw every right-hand throw over the top and every left-hand throw under the hand. The resulting windmill should look like a blur of wheeling hands, with all of the balls revolving around them. If you find that the balls are instead revolving around the under-the-hand ball, however, aim this throw more to the left and the pattern should look better.

28

There are many different ways to discover new tricks or patterns— it's up to you to put them together!

One Up, Two Up

For the next trick, it's essential to know how to juggle two in one hand in columns. One up, two up is not only a useful method of learning two in one hand in columns, but is also in itself a wonderful trick that offers many further juggling variations.

1 Pick up three balls, holding two in your right hand, one in your left.

2 Throw one ball straight up. When it peaks, simultaneously throw the two other balls straight up on either side. Continue the one-up, two-up, one-up, two-up sequence. (When the pattern has become more solid, you will probably notice that your right hand is juggling two in one hand in columns.)

3 If you're feeling really confident, you could try to alternate hands when catching the middle ball.

The reverse cascade involves juggling every ball with both hands every time—very hard!

1

2

29

Variations on the One Up, Two Up

For the next series of variations, you'll need to get a solid, head-height, one up, two up going. If you try to insert some of these tricks into a cascade, you may end up with a whole new juggling routine. Remember to bear the following tips in mind and try to be open-minded when learning new tricks. Most things can be done if you think before you throw, as well as vice versa.

1 Change the positions of the one-up ball and the other balls by juggling the one-up ball either to the left or to the right of the pattern.

2 Change the one-up ball's position every throw, making it go first to the right, then to the middle, and finally to the left.

3 Try occasionally to insert under-the-hand throws using the one-up ball, especially when changing the balls' places in the pattern. You could also try inserting over-the-top throws.

Splitting the Brain

The following trick is really difficult to perform. Throw the one-up ball up into the middle as usual, but instead of throwing up the two-up balls, try a simultaneous crossing throw. Although there's a small risk of collision, it usually works. You could also try catching the balls with your hands crossed and then immediately throw them back in the same direction.

The name of this skill may sound gruesome, but "splitting the brain" actually means doing two things at once, that is, training your hands to work independently. Most commonly used in two-in-one-hand patterns, the easiest way to learn this important skill is to build it up stage by stage.

1 Start by juggling the two-in-one-hand pattern. Now touch your nose with your other hand very slowly. (You'll probably find this difficult.)

2 Carry on juggling and then touch your knee, your foot, or your forehead.

3 Continue juggling while you transfer the balls to your other hand and then repeat the touching exercise.

4 Start juggling two in one hand in columns, using any hand. Hold a third ball in your other hand. Now start moving this third ball in perfect sync with the outermost ball. (This pattern, which resembles one up, two up, is known as the elevator.)

The elevator 1.

The Shower

Once your hands have started to work a little more independently, try the shower pattern. Although you may already have come across it by mistake when using two balls to juggle a cascade, this version is the full-blown, three-ball shower, in which your dominant hand throws high throws to your weaker hand and your weaker hand keeps feeding the balls back to your dominant hand. Note that not only is the pattern harder to learn than the cascade, but it should also be juggled much higher in the air to enable you to maintain a steady rhythm.

1 Start by holding two balls in your dominant hand and one in your weaker hand. Launch the shower by throwing a ball from your dominant hand to your weaker hand. As soon as the first ball peaks, throw the next ball from the same hand in the same way.

2 Your throwing hand now being empty, transfer the ball in your weaker hand to it. Your weaker hand is now ready to take the first catch. So the pattern is set: one hand throws while the other hand catches.

Juggling a Gap

Juggling a gap is a very useful skill when three-ball juggling. A gap is simply a ball that has gone missing, making a hole in the pattern that can be filled with something interesting.

The easiest way to learn the trick is to practice juggling a three-ball cascade using only two balls. You may find this quite difficult at first. If so, try juggling the balls so that they follow each other in a snakelike pattern.

1 Start by holding both balls in your right hand and then throwing them to your left hand, one after the other. Then reverse the pattern. The throwing order is right, right, left, left.

2 You'll find that your hands will sometimes be unoccupied. When this happens, fill the gap by touching your ear. (We'll be juggling the gap in a more interesting way later.)

The elevator 2.

33

The Multiplex

The multiplex involves throwing two balls at the same time, rather than just one. Practice it by throwing up two balls at the same time so that each falls into a different hand. (It's actually a lot easier than it sounds.) You could either insert the multiplex into a running cascade or use it as a starting point by multiplexing two balls and, when they peak, throwing a third one up into the middle before catching the first two balls and then starting to juggle.

A split multiplex is when you throw the balls so that they rise to the same height and then part ways, while a stacked multiplex is when you throw them within the same column (i.e., straight up and then straight down).

The hold for the split multiplex.

Making the throw.

The hold for the stacked multiplex.

37

Making the throw.

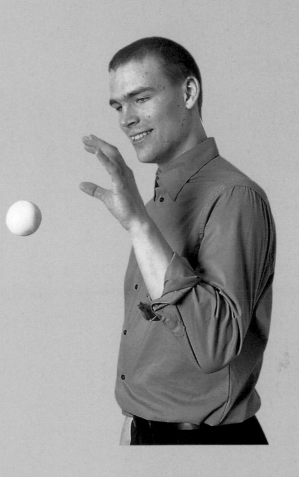

Classic Tricks

Classic Tricks

By now the fundamentals of three-ball juggling should come automatically, and you may even have invented some tricks of your own. In the following section we'll be covering some classic tricks, as well as some more unorthodox moves.

The Machine

If you can perform the elevator, the machine is both easy to learn and impressive.

1 Start juggling two balls in columns using your right hand. The ball in your left hand should move in synchronization with the ball on the farthest right, up and down, up and down.

2 Using your left hand, which should still be moving in synchronization, follow the upward path of the ball on the farthest right, make a sharp turn to the left, and then drop the ball. Quickly return your left hand to its starting position in the bottom left-hand corner of the pattern, clawing the former middle ball as you pull it back.

40

3 Now back in the starting position, keep the pattern continuous, following the rhythm in your mind as you juggle: up, across, back.

Claw

The claw is simply a different way of catching the ball: instead of letting the ball fall into your catching hand, snatch it in midair, with your palm facing downward.

Practice this move as you would practice any other trick, making each stage more difficult. First practice clawing only one ball. Then juggle a cascade and, when a ball peaks, instead of waiting for it to fall, reach up, grab it, and pull it down before throwing it back into the pattern. Once you have managed to claw one ball, move on to clawing two in a row.

Claw technique 1.

With the claw, you snatch the ball out of the air.

Claw technique 2.

42

Yo-yo

This is one of the few juggling tricks that combines juggling and magic because it gives the illusion that an invisible string connects one ball to another. This manouver can be combined with tricks like one up, two up, machine, and right, middle, left.

1 Using your right hand, juggle two in one hand in columns. The ball on the farthest left is the yo-yo ball.

2 Using your left hand, hold a third ball a couple of inches above the yo-yo ball and follow it up and down, so that the balls are moving in synchronization.

3 You can transfer the trick to the other hand by throwing the ball on the farthest right over the top to give the illusion that your right hand is holding the string.

The Contortionist

This trick is not so much a distortion of the cascade as a contortion of the juggler's body. The easiest way is to learn it is to stretch your most flexible arm across your body and then to practice the cascade, one throw at a time. Another way is to throw one high throw, quickly wrap one arm around your back, and then continue the pattern. When learning the contortionist, it's best to point your fingers to the side rather than forward, as this will release some of the tension in your wrists.

Try to transfer the pattern from one side to the other every third throw. The right hand throws a ball across, then catches the incoming ball, and thus the sides are swapped. Once you are happy that you've mastered the cascade in the contortionist's position, try a shower pattern.

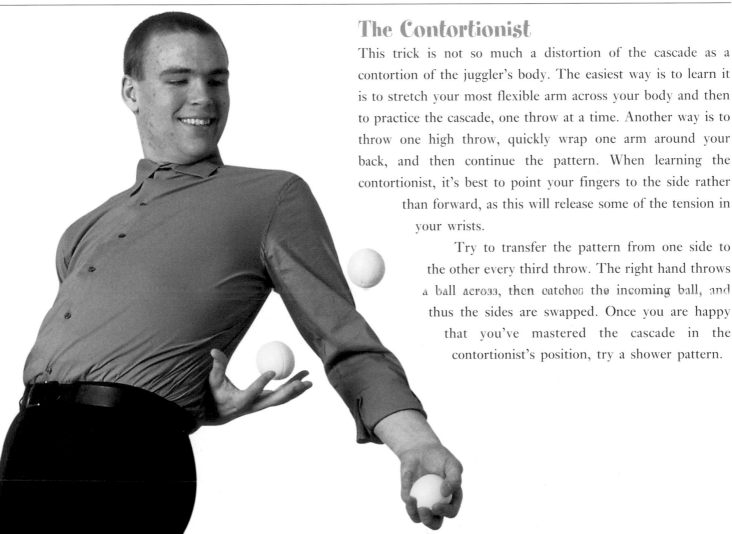

43

Penguin

When juggled smoothly, the penguin looks really hilarious.

1 Start by turning your right hand outward as far as it will go, so that your fingers are pointing to the right. This is the position in which your hand will catch the balls, and you'll then need to untwist it quickly to make the throw.

2 Try making a throw with one ball to see if you can catch it. The secret to a successful catch is to let your arm hang down, thereby preventing the ball from hitting your elbow.

3 Now juggle a cascade in the penguin style—you'll probably find it extremely tricky.

Mills Mess

You won't master this classic three-ball pattern in a day, so take your time.

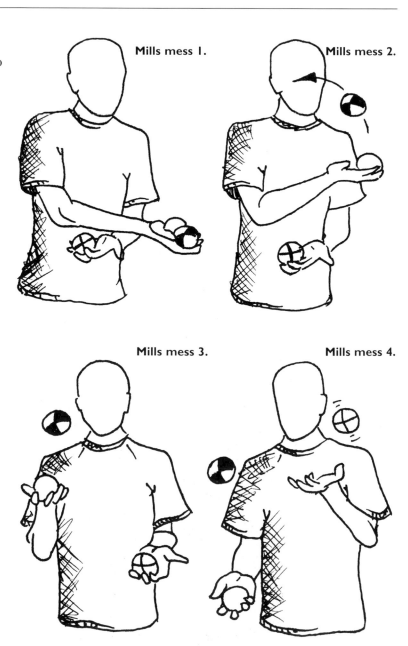

Mills mess 1.

Mills mess 2.

Mills mess 3.

Mills mess 4.

44

One-ball Exercise

Take one ball in your right hand, cross your right arm over your left, throw the ball to the right, uncross your arms, then cross them the other way round and catch the ball in your left hand. The ball and your arms should now have swapped positions. (You can hold the other two balls in your other hand if you like.)

Practice the exercise both ways until you feel happy with it.

Mills mess 1.

Two Balls

Mills mess 2.

1 Take one ball in one hand and two in the other, and cross your right arm over your left. Throw the first ball (the top hand, in this case the right hand, always throws first) to the right and then uncross your arms.

2 Using your left hand, throw the second ball straight upward. Now cross your left arm over your right and catch the first ball. Catch the second ball with your right hand.

3 This is the normal exchange, but with the added feature of crossed and uncrossed arms. If you're having trouble keeping track of which ball's going where, use different-colored balls. Practice this exercise in both directions, always remembering that the top hand throws first.

45

Three Balls

This is the difficult part, so if you get this right, you're halfway there.

Mills mess 3.

Mills mess 4.

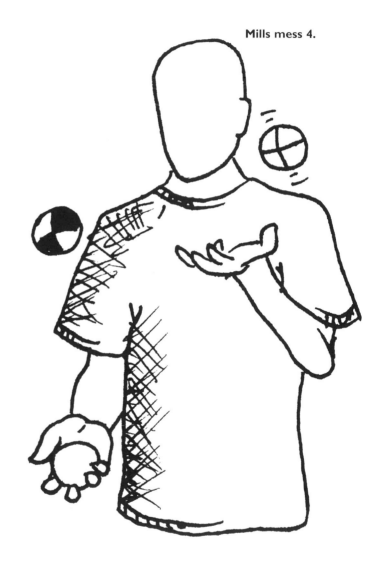

1 Take two balls in your right hand and one in your left hand. Cross your right arm over your left arm. The right hand starts because it is on top. Throw the first ball to the right and uncross your arms. Using your left hand, throw the second ball upward, cross your left arm over your right, and then catch the first ball. (Up to this point it's exactly the same as the two-ball exercise.)

2 The second ball is about to land in your right hand, but because this hand is already holding a ball, it needs to throw that ball over the top of the descending ball, aiming to the right, before catching the second ball. Your right arm should still be in the same place, under the left arm. Use your left hand to catch the over-the-top ball. Your left arm should now be over your right arm and your left hand should be holding two balls.

3 Practice this pattern the other way round until you feel that you've mastered it.

Mills mess 5.

Changing Directions

The full-blown Mills-mess pattern is a six-beat pattern consisting of three throws in each direction. This is how to put the throws together: when the third ball is about to land in the top hand (which is already holding a ball), it should trigger the first throw in the next sequence of three throws. The held ball is the first to be thrown, in the opposite direction to the incoming ball.

Over the Head

Juggling over your head isn't as hard as you may think. Most novice three-ballers are capable of juggling the cascade in this way after an hour or so's practice. Once you've mastered the technique, it offers a range of possible variations, and most patterns (including Mills mess) can be juggled over the head.

You could try to juggle the cascade in a really low (about knee height) and tight pattern, throwing one ball high into the air and then resuming the cascade above your head. If you're juggling bouncing balls, you could also try to bounce one ball on your forehead before continuing the cascade. If you keep your elbows pointing outward, rather than forward, you can juggle like this for hours.

The Box

The box, the last trick in this intermediate section, has both an interesting shape and features a new throwing technique. One ball will rise and fall in a column to the right, another ball will do the same to the left, while a third ball will switch from side to side beneath them. You will be throwing two balls with both hands at the same time, but in different directions.

3 To perform the full pattern, pick up two balls in your right hand and one in your left hand. Start by throwing a ball from your right hand straight upward and proceed as before. From now on, when the right-hand ball's peaking, throw an "L" shape to the left, followed by an "L" shape to the right. That's all there is to it.

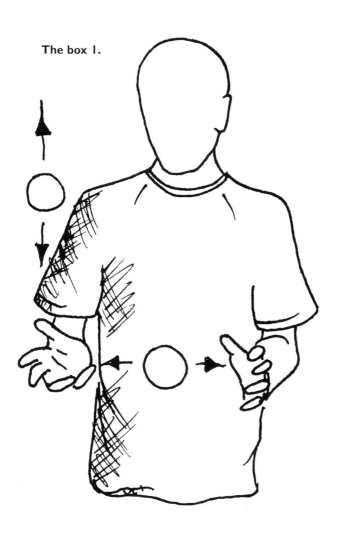

The box 1.

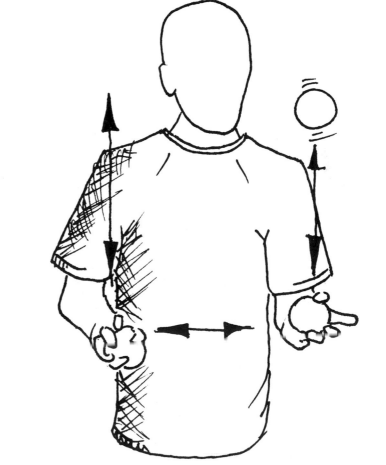

The box 2.

1 Start off by throwing one ball horizontally back and forth between your hands a couple of times.

2 Now take one ball in each hand. Your left hand is going to throw its ball straight across to your right hand at the same time as your right hand is throwing its ball straight upward. When the right-hand ball peaks, throw the horizontal ball back in the same direction with your right hand, so that you catch the balls at the same time. The pattern should look like an upside-down "L." Practice throwing "L" shapes on both sides before moving on. (Note that this may take some time and that you'll find it quite hard.)

Adding More Balls

Adding More Balls

Juggling four balls is as easy as juggling two in one hand—albeit simultaneously in both hands—this pattern, called fountain, being the simplest four-ball pattern. And when juggling four-ball patterns has become second nature, try your hand at five-ball juggling.

Juggling With Four Balls

In order to learn four-ball juggling, you must first have mastered two things: juggling two balls in your right hand and juggling two balls in your left. Thereafter, the difficult part is doing both at the same time.

Practice four-ball juggling for two to three weeks, and at the end of this period you should be able to make around fifty catches.

1 Holding two balls in each hand, throw up one ball from each hand at the same time. When the first balls peak, throw the second pair of balls up the middle before catching the first two balls and then the last two. Continuing to use both hands, see if you can keep this pattern going.

2 You'll probably notice that the two individual patterns appear to attract each other, moving closer and closer to each other until they collide in the middle. To solve this problem, face the edge of an open door, so that your right hand is on one side and your left is on the other, and then start juggling the four balls.

3 With or without the door, the chances are that you won't feel comfortable juggling the four-ball pattern. This is because it is asynchronous, that is, your hands take it in turns to make the throws. The following tips may help: firstly, always try to launch the pattern with your weakest hand; secondly, if the patterns become twisted, don't just adjust your hands, instead follow the pattern with your whole body; and, thirdly, finish by throwing a high ball.

Juggling With Five Balls

Be warned: learning to juggle with five balls is very hard and will continue to be so even after you've mastered it, which will probably take about six months. However, if you have a positive attitude, five beanbags, and lots of time and patience, you will eventually be able to juggle this high, fast, and wild cascade pattern.

There are a number of exercises that you will need to learn and practice before you have even a hope of successfully launching yourself into the full five-ball pattern. Some are quite easy, others are harder, and some are positively nightmarish. Because your brain has not yet been trained to cope with five moving objects, we'll start with three.

The Three-ball Flash

1 Take two balls in your right hand and one in your left, then throw them upward in rapid succession, cascade style. When they peak, clap your hands before catching all of the balls.

2 An easier method is to juggle a cascade, throwing the balls into the air at about three times their normal height, then to clap your hands once (and preferably twice) before continuing the cascade as normal. The handclaps will later be replaced by two balls.

54

For the three-ball shower, you need to keep the balls really high.

The Three-ball Shower

Because the throws used in the three-ball shower (see page 33) are exactly the same as the throws used in the five-ball cascade, it's essential to have mastered this pattern. Practice the shower both ways, keeping the pattern really high (about three times the height of a normal three-ball cascade), until you are confident that you can juggle it.

The Snake

An attractive pattern in itself, the snake is one of the cornerstones of five-ball juggling. Practice it every day, but in only in short bursts to prevent yourself from becoming bored with it.

1 Take three balls in your right hand and throw them to your left hand one after the other (throw the last one when the first ball lands).

2 Immediately throw the balls back to your right hand in the same way, so that they look like they are chasing each other in a snakelike movement (see right).

The Four-ball Crossover

The four-ball crossover comprises the first four throws of the five-ball cascade.

1 Take two balls in each hand and start as if you were juggling a three-ball flash (see page 54), the only difference being that you're throwing four balls instead of three. The pattern is: right, left, right, left (your hands are then empty for a split second), catch, catch, catch, and catch. The balls have now been transferred from one hand to the other.

2 Try juggling the four-ball crossover the other way around as well. Carry on practicing with four balls until you feel confident, then move on to five balls.

Five-ball Juggling

Although juggling with five balls may seem daunting, it won't be so difficult if you have practiced and mastered the previous exercises. It will, however, still take a long time for your hands and brain to adjust to juggling five balls, so have patience, practice a lot, and add a few more throws and catches to the pattern each week. Do this, and one day you'll find yourself juggling ten catches and then even fifteen (but no doubt you'll stick at this figure for some time thereafter).

1 Pick up five balls and try to flash them so that you make five throws, five catches, and a clean finish.

2 Preferably standing in front of a bed (so that you can pick up any dropped balls easily), throw all five balls so that they cross in the middle and then try to catch them again. You'll probably find this rather difficult, but if you start slowly and let the balls fall onto the bed before speeding up your throws, you'll find yourself improving.

57

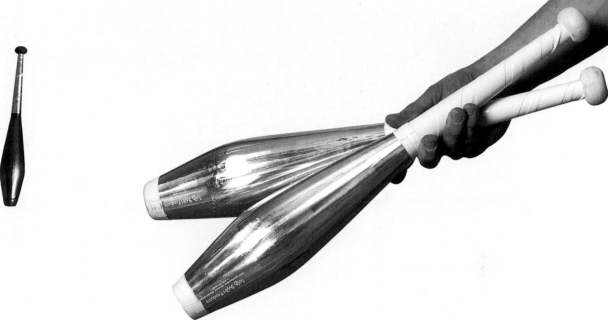

Club-juggling

Club-juggling

Having mastered juggling with balls, the next step is to move on to clubs. Club-jugglers have a lot of fun, even though their clubs are expensive and take up a lot of room—-both when stored in a bag and when flying through the air—-while a blow inflicted by the handle of a club can be far more painful than being hit by a stray beanbag. To start with, we'll be using three clubs, as well as a couple of beanbags.

The Single Spin

Juggling with three clubs is about as difficult as juggling with three balls and will take roughly the same amount of time to learn. The pattern is the same and, apart from the props themselves, the only thing that you'll find different is learning how to control the spin.

Single spin 1.

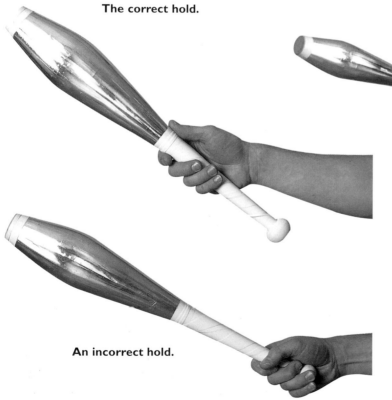

The correct hold.

An incorrect hold.

1 Start by holding one club as you would a frying pan, with your thumb on the tape. Once you're happy with your grip, try throwing the club from one hand to the other a few times.

2 Experiment with throws of different height, speed, and spin until you start to become used to the feel of your new props. For example, give your club one full spin while throwing it into the air and then catching it. Try throwing it up high while giving it an even, slow spin or throwing it really low, using a quick spin. Catch it in the same hand that threw it or throw it across to your other hand.

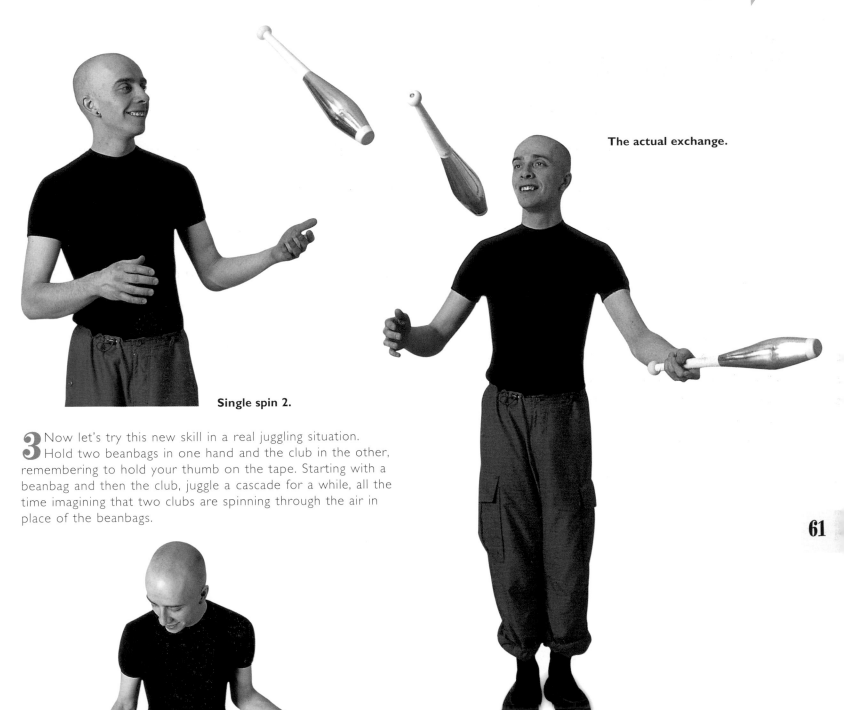

The actual exchange.

Single spin 2.

3 Now let's try this new skill in a real juggling situation. Hold two beanbags in one hand and the club in the other, remembering to hold your thumb on the tape. Starting with a beanbag and then the club, juggle a cascade for a while, all the time imagining that two clubs are spinning through the air in place of the beanbags.

61

4 Next we'll practice the exchange. Note that it's almost impossible to throw a club without generating some momentum first, and the ideal starting position is to hold the clubs pointing away from your body at an angle of about 45°. Now take a club in each hand and throw them as you did when you were learning to exchange balls (see page 17). The second club should go under the first, and don't forget to perform a scooping motion before you throw it—when one club is thrown, the other one should swing down to make the scoop. Don't forget to practice this exercise using both of your hands.

Exchange – starting position.

Circus or Normal?

Jugglers have their own jargon, and when you're holding two clubs in one hand, your starting position is said to be either "circus" or "normal." Take two clubs in your right hand, making the handles cross, and look at your hand. Is the club on the left on top of the other one? If so, you are using the normal grip. If the club on the left is under the other club, however, you are using the circus grip. In either case, the club on the left is thrown first.

Practice making a couple of throws with the clubs using both starting positions to see which suits you best. Once you're happy with your grip, practice starting and stopping in this position until it's become second nature.

Circus grip.

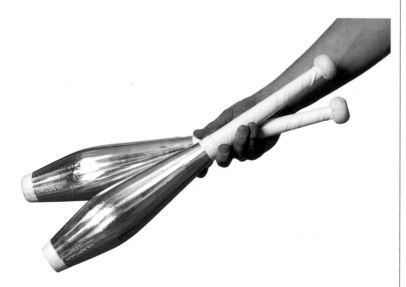

Normal grip.

The Three-club Cascade

Juggling a three-club cascade is not as difficult as you may think. It will take you some time to perform a smooth cascade consistently, but after a few days of practicing hard, you should succeed.

1 Take two clubs in your right hand and one in your left, using the grip that you find the most comfortable (most jugglers prefer the normal grip).

2 Perform three throws and three catches. If you end up catching all of the clubs, you can start to call yourself a club-juggler.

Performing Tricks With Clubs

You should always try to push yourself when juggling, and once you can regularly perform a three-club cascade, it's time to start working on some tricks. As when learning to juggle balls, mastering some club tricks is essential to your progress. The most important thing is to be able to control a club's spin, and in a few tricks the spin itself is the trick.

Double Spin

First of all, try performing this trick with one club by throwing it so that it turns twice in the air before catching it. Although mastering this double spin may take some practice—at first, all that you'll see is a wheeling blur—after a while you will acquire the knack. Some jugglers watch the knob of the club as it turns in the air, while others simply insert their hand into the midst of the blur and hope for the best.

When you feel that you have learned this skill, try juggling a three-club cascade and throwing a double-spinning club into it. While the double-spinning club is floating through the air, you will be holding onto the other two clubs, which means that you can focus on the double-spinning club before returning it to the cascade.

Once you've mastered throwing one double-spinning club into the cascade, you could try double-spinning two clubs in a row or even juggling the entire cascade with double-spinning clubs.

Throwing a high double.

The Return of the Two in One Hand

Juggling two in one hand with clubs is much harder than with balls, particularly since it's almost impossible to juggle using single-spinning clubs.

The easiest way is to learn it is to start juggling a three-club cascade and then to throw a double-spinning club from your strongest hand more or less straight up; when it's peaking, throw another double-spinning club from the same hand, rolling-out style, before resuming the cascade.

Practice juggling clubs in the two-in-one-hand pattern using both hands until you feel confident that you can perform the trick smoothly and successfully.

63

Club-passing

Club-passing

Although club-juggling is like any other style of juggling in that there are different ways of juggling clubs and a wide range of tricks to be performed with them, they have one clear advantage: they're far better than balls for passing between partners. Because clubs are so expensive, try to find someone to practice with who owns their own clubs. If your cascades are solid enough, you should be able to learn the standard passing pattern in one afternoon.

Preparing for the Four Count

The standard pattern for club-passing is the four count (sometimes also referred to as "every other"). The cascade of club-passing, the basic pattern is a pass and three self-throws, giving you time to recover from a bad pass before making the next. Before attempting the four count, practice the following exercises with a partner.

First exercise 1.

1 Start your practice session with one club. There will be only two different throws in this exercise: a self-throw and a pass. Stand facing each other, about 3 meters (roughly 10 feet) apart, holding the club in your left hand. Giving it a single spin, throw it to your right hand and then toss it across —again giving it a single spin—to your partner's left hand, which should be held in a vertical catching position. After pausing for a few seconds, your partner should then return the club to you in the same way. Practice the exchange a few times.

First exercise 2.

2 Now pick up another club so that you are holding one club in each hand. Starting with the left-hand club, give it a single spin and throw it toward your right hand, at which point your right hand should clear itself by passing the club that it is holding to your partner's left hand. Pause for a second before throwing the club in your right hand to your partner's left hand as your partner clears it with a self-throw to his or her right hand. Your partner should now be holding both clubs. Practice this exchange until you're passing comfortably.

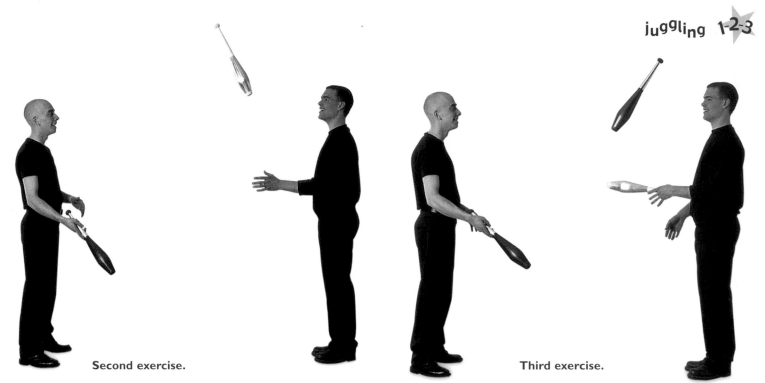

Second exercise.

Third exercise.

3 The three around is a useful pattern when learning difficult tricks. Take hold of a club in each hand, while your partner grasps a club in his or her left hand. Giving it a single spin, throw the left-hand club to your right hand as your right hand gives the club that it is holding a single spin while throwing it across to your partner's left hand, your partner clearing his or her left hand with a self-throw to his or her right hand. Your partner should now be holding two clubs and you should be holding the third club in your right hand. Start again by passing the club in your right hand to your partner's

left hand as your partner throws a self-throw and then a pass, and so on. Remember that it's always the last club that is thrown first, triggering off the passing of the rest of the clubs.

4 Next, try passing a running three-club cascade to your partner by juggling the cascade and then passing all three clubs to your partner by making three consecutive throws from your right hand. Your partner should juggle them for a while before passing them back.

The Four Count

Stand facing each other while juggling a synchronized three-club cascade; every other right-hand throw, pass a club from your right hand to your partner's left, your left hand at the same time receiving one of your partner's clubs. The four count's alternative name, "every other," refers to the pass that is made every other right-hand throw.

With both of you holding two clubs in your right hand and one in your left, stand facing each other. Simultaneously raise your right hands (ready), then lower them (steady), and start by passing a club to your partner's left hand (go!) Catch the incoming club, juggle three self-throws, and then make the next pass.

As you juggle, say the rhythm out loud: "Pass, two, three, four. Pass, two, three, four." The "pass" is always made from the right hand, the "two" is always from the left hand, the "three" is from the right hand, and the "four," triggering off the next pass, is from the left hand.

After a couple of rounds you'll start to get a feel for

each other's throwing technique. It's common to try to compensate for your partner's bad passes by responding to overspun incoming clubs with underspun passes, while if your partner juggles very slowly, it's probably because you're juggling too quickly. Don't be afraid to call out helpful hints to each other as you juggle.

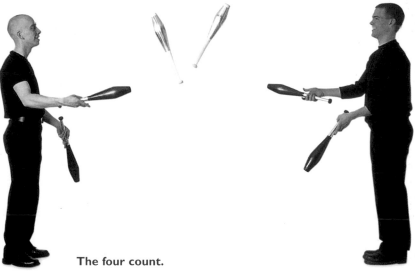

The four count.

The Three Count

You'll need to be ambidextrous to master the three-count pattern. And although this pattern is hard to learn because the passes and catches are made with both hands, you'll become a better juggler for it. Not only will your juggling become more balanced, but you'll also develop passing and catching skills using both of your hands.

Start as if you were going to juggle a four count—up, down, go—and make the first throw a pass. From now on, the pattern will be pass, two, three, pass, two, three. The first pass should be made with the right hand as before, followed by two self-throws, and the second pass should be made with the left hand.

Up.

Down.

Go.

Launch.

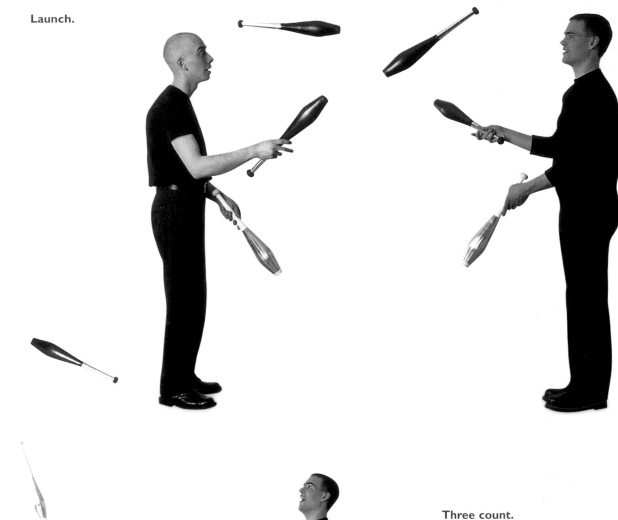

Three count.

The Two Count

You'll be relieved to know that the two count is easier than the three count. Like the four count, this is a right-hand pattern, so you don't have to worry about tricky left-hand passes.

Simply juggle the pattern as you would a four count, but make every right-hand throw a pass, so that the order runs pass, self-throw, pass, self-throw, pass, self-throw.

The One Count

There is no room for self-throws (or mistakes) in the one count (also known as the ultimates). Every right- and left-hand throw is a pass, the pattern running as follows: up, down, go! Pass, pass, pass, pass . . . The one count should look as though two separate cascades are being juggled between your right hand and your partner's left and your left hand and your partner's right.

Dealing With Dropped Clubs

Although you will inevitably drop a lot of clubs when you're club-juggling, the good thing is that you can recover more gracefully than if you were juggling solo. The secret is not to stop juggling and to keep the rhythm in your head: pass, two, three, four, pass, oops! three, four. You may be holding two clubs, while a third has clattered to the floor, but you still have the rhythm in your head. Pass! Always pass! Even if you're not juggling! Your partner may still be juggling, and when they pass a club to you they will expect one back, so oblige them. Although you will still end up holding two clubs, you now have three beats in which to pick up your dropped club, grip it comfortably, prepare yourself mentally, and then pass, two, three, four, and you'll be up and running again.

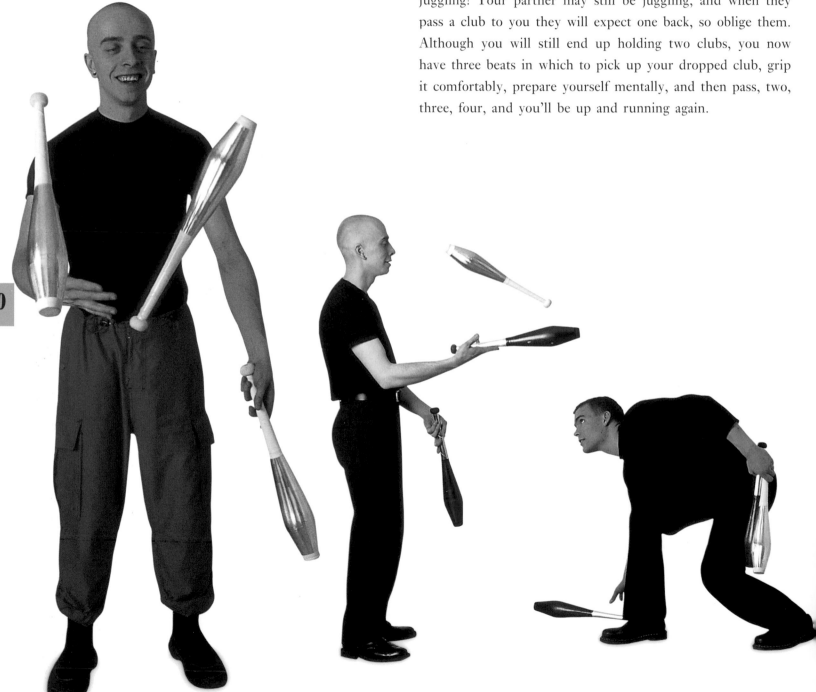

Routines

When juggling the four-, three-, two-, and one-count patterns, you'll often find yourself juggling until you drop. If you want to feel that you're making progress, however, you need to set yourself a goal to achieve. There are many juggling routines that have a beginning, middle, and end to try, including the 3-3-10 and the harder 4-4-8.

The 3-3-10

The 3-3-10, which starts off slowly before becoming harder, is an ideal routine for right-handed beginners to learn. You'll be juggling three rounds of a six count, then three rounds of a four count, before finishing off with ten rounds of a two count.

Start with an up, down, go, and then juggle the routine as follows in the box, right.

Pass, two, three, four, five, six (the numbers are self-throws)

Pass, two, three, four, five, six.

Pass, two, three, four, five, six.

Pass, two, three, four.

Pass, two, three, four.

Pass, two, three, four.

Pass, two.

Pass, two.

Pass, two.

Pass, two.

Pass, two.

Pass, two.

Pass, two.

Pass, two.

Pass, two.

Pass, two.

If you're feeling confident, finish off with a really high triple self-throw and catch it before taking a bow.

The 4-4-8

Harder than the 3-3-10, the 4-4-8 uses both right- and left-hand passes, and the grand finale is nightmarish.

The patterns consist of four rounds of a five count, four rounds of a three count, and eight rounds of a one count, that is, eight passes in a row, from both hands.

Starting with your right hand, juggle the 4-4-8 as follows.

Pass, two, three, four, five.
Pass, two, three, four, five.
Pass, two, three, four, five.
Pass, two, three, four, five.
Pass, two, three.
Pass, two, three.
Pass, two, three.
Pass, two, three.
Pass.
Pass.
Pass.
Pass.
Pass.
Pass.
Pass.
Pass.

Finish off the set with a high triple self-throw and a pirouette —or any other manouvers that you prefer—and then pat yourself on the back.

Syncopations

Syncopations are a way of playing around with the rhythm of a pattern. They are easy to learn, need no rehearsal, and also look impressive. The easiest way of learning them is inserting them into a running four count.

Early Double

If you think about it, when you actually throw a club to your partner doesn't really concern them as long as they receive it on the correct beat and in the correct hand. Bearing this in mind, during a running four count, and using your left hand, aim a club at your partner's catching hand on the "four" beat, giving it a double spin as you throw it. In other words, instead of throwing it to your right hand and then passing it to your partner, you throw it directly to their catching hand, giving it a double spin to enable it to spend more time in the air and prevent it from landing early.

73

Late Double

This syncopation is a little harder for your partner, although your side of the pattern remains more or less the same as in the early double.

When juggling a normal four-count pattern, the club leaves your hand and arrives in your partner's left hand before being passed to their right hand. Instead of passing the club to your partner's catching hand (the left one), pass it straight to their right hand, using a double-spin throw to make up for the missed beat. Count the beats out loud, to avoid losing the rhythm while your partner is standing holding two clubs and waiting for the incoming pass.

Self-throws

Another syncopation is to alter your side of the pattern only. One way of doing this is making a syncopated self-throw, a double self-throw with the right hand, as follows.

1. Pass with your right hand.

2. Throw from your left hand to your right.

3. Throw a double self-throw from your right hand, which then catches the "two" club.

4. As the double self-throw starts to descend, prepare to catch it by clearing your right hand with a pass.

Trick Passes

Tomahawk step 1.

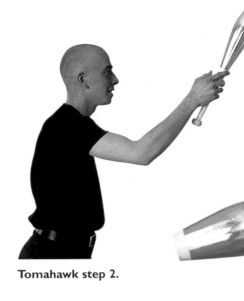

Tomahawk step 2.

Spear.

As soon as you're confidently juggling a basic four count, you're ready to start experimenting with trick passes, some of which are really easy, while others are more difficult. A good way to learn the more tricky ones is to use the three around (see page 67) as a practice pattern; the last club to be thrown is the practice club.

In one of the easiest trick passes, under the leg, you simply throw a club under your right (or left) leg as you pass it to your partner. You may find passing a club between your legs without lifting your feet off the ground rather harder, however.

Fish.

Under the leg step 2.

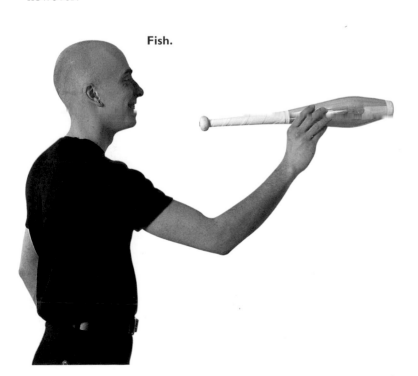

Under the leg step 1.

A club that is thrown to your partner without any spin is called a "flat," while a "buzzsaw" is a club that spins violently through the air. A club that is thrown so that it flies through the air like a dart is called a "spear" if the fatter end of the club is at the front, otherwise being called a "fish." A club that is thrown as you would an ax or a knife is called a tomahawk; always try to aim low when making this kind of pass, and remember that it looks more impressive if it's thrown with a double spin.

Another entertaining thing that you can try when passing clubs is to catch your partner's incoming club in your left hand, transfer it to your right hand (which should now be holding two clubs), and then, with your arms pointing outward from your body, twirl a pirouette, always following the underlying rhythm in your head, starting to pass again when the pirouette comes to an end.

Robin Hood.

Leg throw.

Pincer pass step 1.

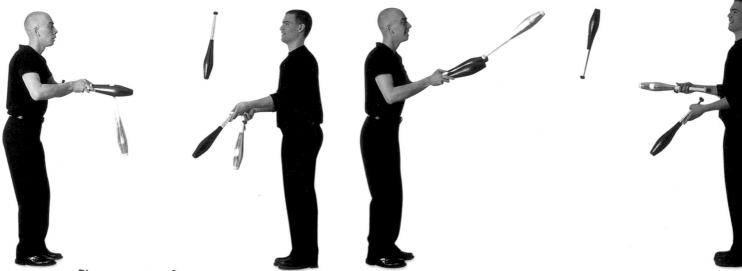

Pincer pass step 2.

Pincer pass step 3.

More Jugglers, More Fun

Another way of livening up club-passing is to include more people in the action. The most common pattern for three club-jugglers is called "feed," which goes something like this.

1 Three jugglers arrange themselves in a rough triangle, two standing next to each other (the feedees) and the other (the feeder) facing them. The feeder will juggle a two count, passing to the feedees in turn. The two feedees will juggle a four count, out of phase with each other, each passing to the feeder.

2 All of the jugglers start off with an "up, down, go." The feeder throws the first pass to the juggler to the right, while juggler to the left juggles two self-passes. From now on, the feeder, using a two count, alternates between the two feedees, while the feedees carry on juggling a normal four count with the feeder.

Running Feed

The natural progression to the feed is the running feed, in which three jugglers take it in turns to be the feeder. The juggler to the left of the feeder is the runner, the juggler to the right then becoming the new feeder.

The runner juggles a four count as normal, while waiting for the incoming pass, starts running and catches the club while running, then positioning him- or herself to the right of the feeder before turning around and passing the next club to the new feeder.

The Box

In the box, four jugglers (two pairs) arrange themselves in a cross or box shape and juggle a four count between the pairs. You can experiment with many patterns in the box: 3-3-10, for example, a couple of syncopations, or even some trick throws. The entertaining part is avoiding the clubs colliding in the middle of the box, although sadly it's no pattern for spectators.

Contact-juggling

Contact-juggling

Imagine this scenario. With music playing in the background, a black-clothed juggler suddenly materializes on the stage in front of you. The juggler produces a medium-sized crystal ball and starts to play with it. The ball seems to float in midair as it slowly rolls from one hand to another before rolling off the juggler's elbow and dropping onto the back of his hand.

80

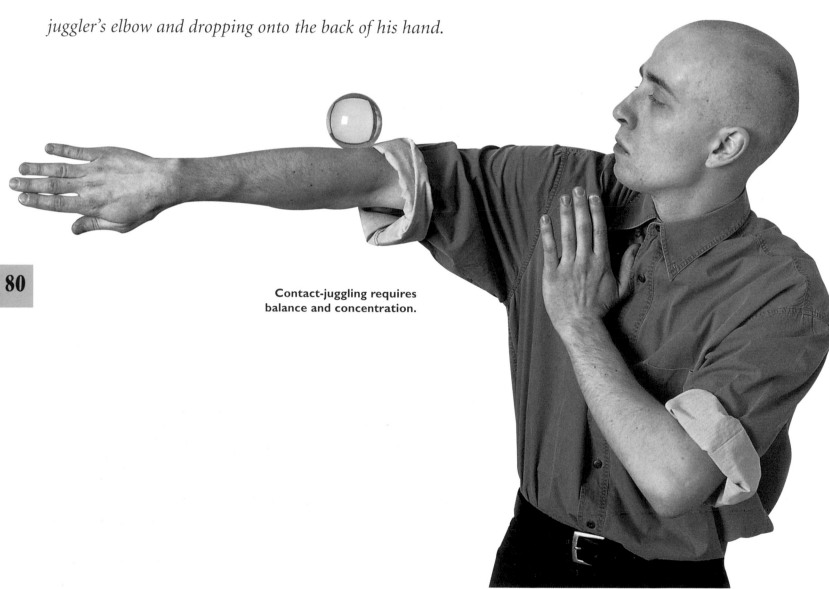

Contact-juggling requires balance and concentration.

The juggler's hand starts to make circlelike movements beneath the ball, which remains perfectly still. As he lifts the ball higher and higher in the air, his hand forms a cage on top of which the balls rests. He makes a quick move and the ball is now trapped inside the cage. The juggler laughs, tosses the ball into the air, catches it on his forehead, turns a very slow pirouette, and exits the stage. This is an example of the art of contact-juggling.

The smooth movements of contact-juggling can be mesmerizing.

At its highest level, contact-juggling can take many years of hard practice to perfect, and although some simple moves can be a pleasure to watch, they also require a lot of practice to master. Indeed, you can never practice contact-juggling too much. The advantage, however, is that you can practice it almost anywhere: in front of the television, for instance, on the bus, or at a boring lecture.

If you've been using beanbags to juggle with until now, you'll need some new props: a ball that is slightly larger than a beanbag—preferably a plastic stage ball—and three or four pool balls for multiple-ball work.

The Butterfly

The first move to learn is called the butterfly, in which the ball travels from your palm to the back of your hand via your middle finger while your hand performs a wavelike motion from right to left. The butterfly is the basis for all contact-juggling moves—it's the contact-juggler's equivalent to the cascade. Unlike the cascade, however, it won't give you the instant satisfaction of seeing yourself improve by the hour and takes weeks of practice before it even starts to look good.

1 Pick up a ball in your right hand. Rest it on your palm, with your fingers pointing to the right. Bounce the ball up and down a few times to accustom yourself to the weight of the ball, then pitch it up in the air and let it come to rest in your palm again. The angle of your arm may feel a bit unnatural, but you'll soon get used to it. Practice pitching the ball upward and then catching it.

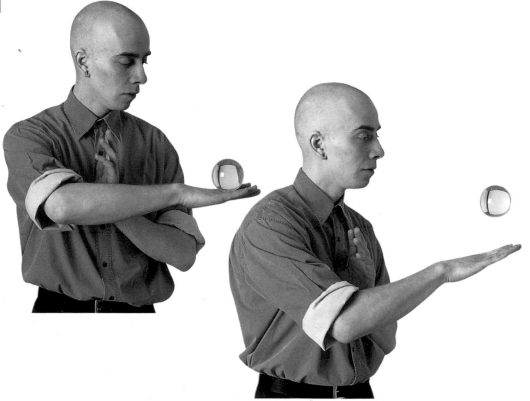

2 Change the position of your hand so that it is facing palm downward and your fingers are pointing to the left. Place the ball on top of your hand in front of the first knuckle of the middle finger so that it rests between your index and ring fingers. (This grip is known as the cradle, and you'll make a steadier cradle if you're holding your middle finger a little lower than the other fingers.) Try to pitch and catch the ball in this position a few times.

The two positions described in steps 1 and 2 are the butterfly's starting and stopping positions. The move itself is a smooth transition of the ball from the first to the second position, during which it should never leave your hand.

Step 3.

Step 4.

3 This exercise is designed to help you get your timing right. Try to pitch the ball from one position to another, from the palm to the cradle and back again, without dropping it.

4 Next we'll try a rolling pitch. Balancing the ball in your palm, roll it to the top of your middle finger, pitch it into the air, and then catch it in the cradle position. Then practice it the other way around by balancing the ball on the back of your hand, rolling it to the top of your middle finger, pitching it upward, and then catching it in your palm. As the ball moves, your hand should be making a wavelike motion beneath it.

5 The final step is to perform the butterfly without the ball being airborne. In one smooth motion, roll the ball from your palm to the cradle via the tip of your middle finger and then back again. When you have perfected the butterfly, the ball should describe a figure of eight while your hand is in constant motion. Practice this step using both of your hands.

83

Butterfly 1.   **Butterfly 2.**   **Butterfly 3.**

Transitions

Learning transitions is the next step for the contact-juggler. Art forms in themselves, these are ways of transferring the ball from one hand to the other without interrupting the motion, smooth motions after all being what contact-juggling is all about.

The simplest transition is the aptly named palm-to-palm transfer. When the ball comes to rest in your palm, with your fingers pointing outward, twist your hand so that you are holding the ball as if you were about to juggle it. Now put your hands together and let the ball roll from one palm to the other in one fluid motion. Next, twist the hand holding the ball so that your fingers point outward again and butterfly the ball. Practice this transition in one single move, without letting the ball come to rest.

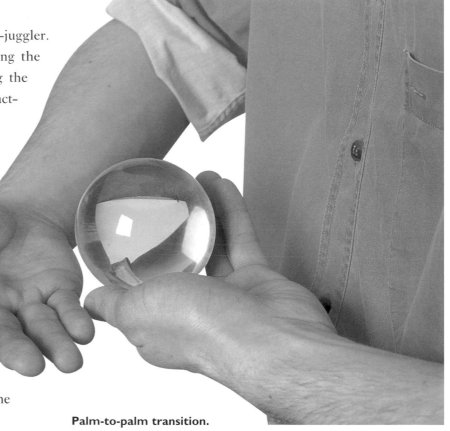

Palm-to-palm transition.

Back-to-back transition.

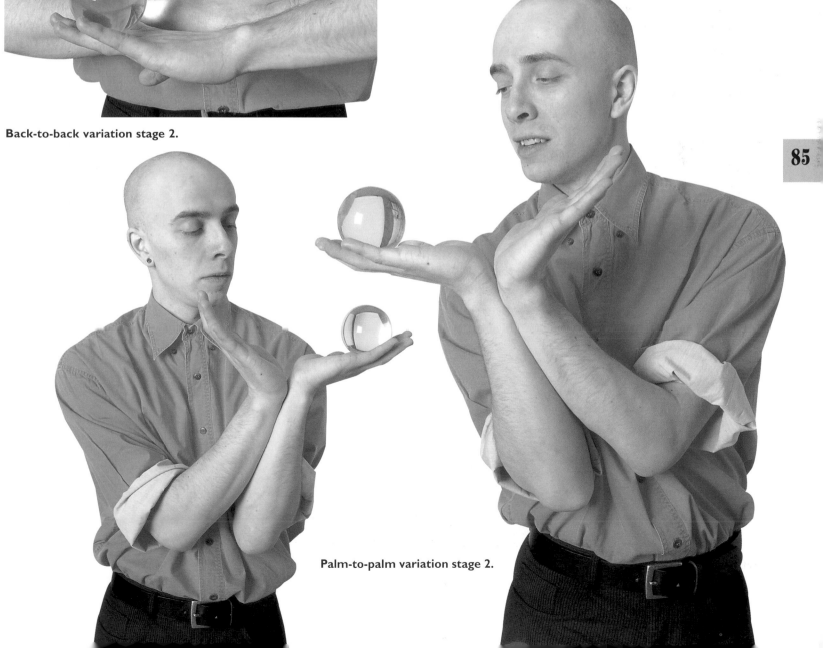

Back-to-back variation stage 4.

Back-to-back variation stage 2.

The back-to-back transfer is a more elegant transition. First, butterfly the ball so that it ends up in the cradle position, then let it roll away from you, over your ring and little fingers, so that it falls off into the cradle made by your other hand.

The most beautiful of the back-to-back transfers is performed slightly differently, however. Again, butterfly the ball so that it ends up in a cradle, letting it roll toward the back of your hand and then over the back of your other hand into the cradle position. The ball should now have enough momentum for your other hand to take it straight into the butterfly move. Although this may appear easy on paper, it's actually a really difficult manouver that will take a lot of practice to perfect.

Palm-to-palm variation stage 2.

85

Palm-to-palm variation stage 2.

Multiple Transitions

There are many different possible combinations of transitions, and one that blends well with the back-to-back transfer is a variation of the palm-to-palm transition. When the ball ends up in your palm, place your hands together—more specifically,

place your wrists together—and let the ball roll from one palm to the other. Bend your fingers upward in this position so that they resemble a cage and let the ball turn a full loop.

One impressive transition is the palm-to-back-to-back-to-palm transfer. Start with the ball resting in the palm of either

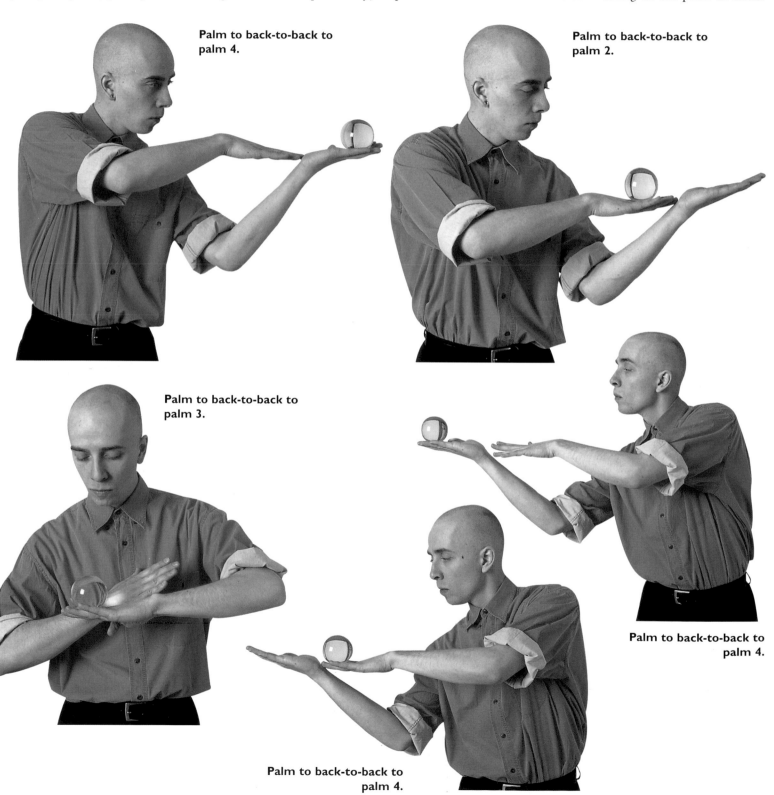

Palm to back-to-back to palm 4.

Palm to back-to-back to palm 2.

Palm to back-to-back to palm 3.

Palm to back-to-back to palm 4.

Palm to back-to-back to palm 4.

hand and your fingers pointing outward. Now roll the ball toward your wrist, catching it in a cradle. Perform a back-to-back transfer and then finish by rolling the ball toward the tip of your middle finger before catching it in your palm.

In the tricky palm-to-back-to-back-to-back-to-back-to-palm transition, the trickiest transfer is the last back transfer. To perform this, make the tips of your middle fingers meet, roll the ball over this rather unstable bridge, and then continue as usual. This move looks particularly impressive if you follow the ball's movement with your whole body.

The trickiest back-to-back exchange.

87

The Cage

The cage resembles the butterfly, except that the ball should come to a halt between your middle and index fingers rather than in the cradle grip. Make the fingertips of both of your hands meet to form a cage, with the ball balancing on top, before quickly turning the cage so that the ball rolls over smoothly to the other hand. (You'll find it easier if you raise

The cage 1.

The cage 2.

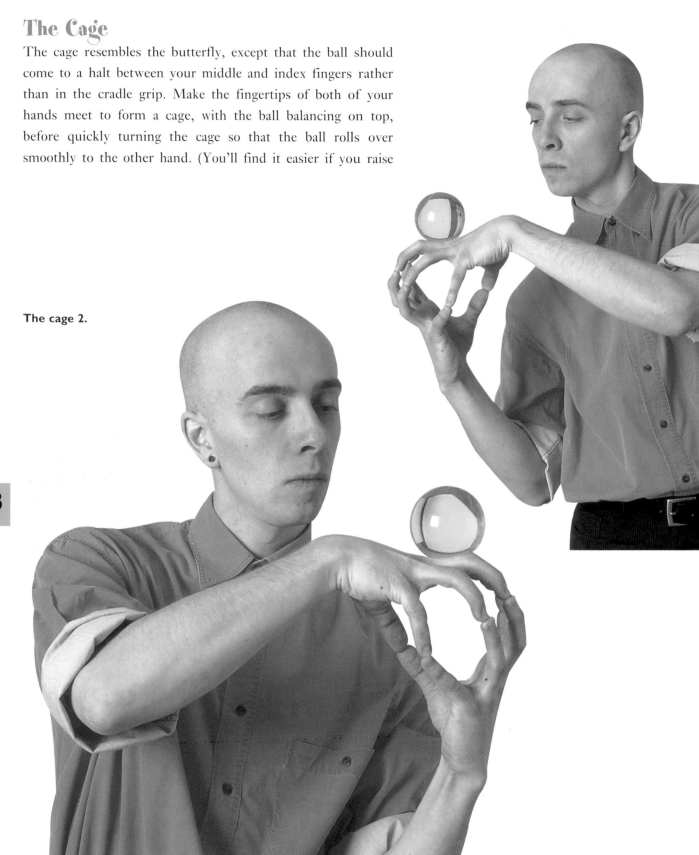

Flattened hands.

both hands when performing this move.) There are many different ways of trapping the ball inside the cage, of which the middle-finger transfer is the easiest. Flatten your hands so that your palms meet, place your middle fingers next to each other, and then roll the ball toward your fingertips. When it reaches the tip of the lower middle finger, roll it back and form the cage again. To get the ball out of the cage, try twisting your hands sideways, thereby making the ball roll between your thumb and middle finger to the top of the cage.

Another continuing transfer is one in which the ball rolls away from you. Perform it by continually rolling the ball off the back of your hand and then catching it on top of your other hand. You could vary this transition by using some palm catches and could also let the ball roll along the whole length of your underarm. Try to keep the ball still while your hands move beneath it, a manouver that is called an isolation.

Catching the ball.

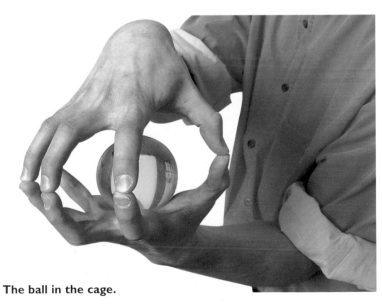

The ball in the cage.

Isolations

The magic that you are trying to evoke when performing isolations involves holding the ball completely still while your hand moves underneath it. Although the ball is actually spinning on its own axis, if you're using an acrylic ball, neither you nor your audience will notice it. This is one of the reasons why isolations look stunning when performed with an acrylic ball, but I recommend that you use an ordinary stage ball when you are practicing.

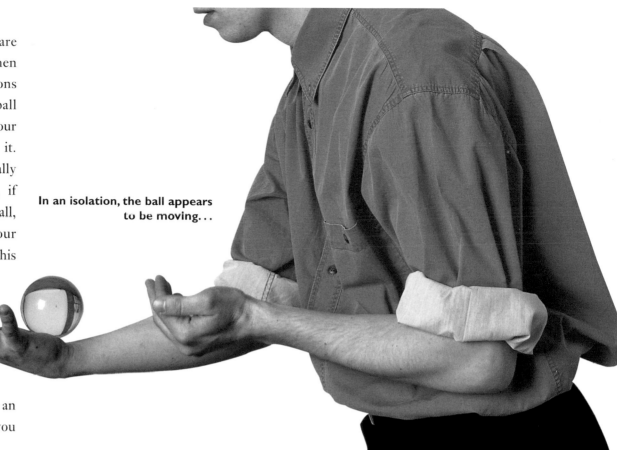

In an isolation, the ball appears to be moving...

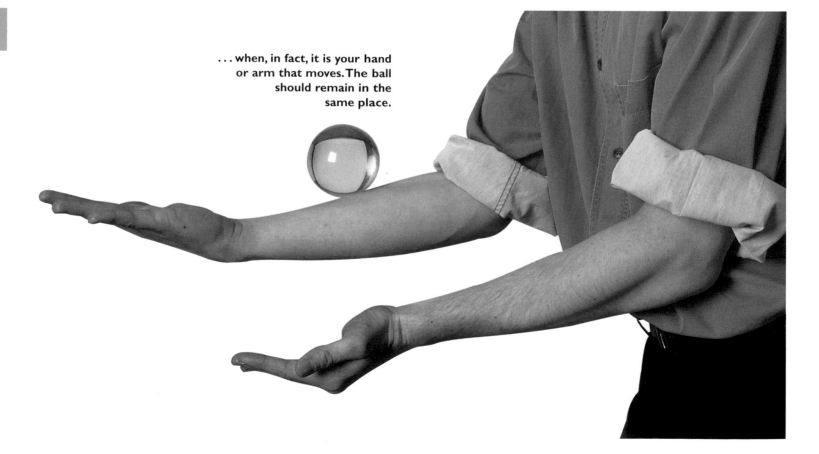

...when, in fact, it is your hand or arm that moves. The ball should remain in the same place.

One of the simplest isolations is to hold the ball between your thumb and middle finger and then to twist your hand while keeping the ball in the same place. It can be quite hard to keep the ball still at first, and a helpful tip is to focus on a object behind it and to align the ball with this object, keeping both fixed together in your line of vision as you perform the manouver. Really show off the ball—by twisting your hand so that the ball is underneath it, over it, and to the side of it—and you can convince yourself that it is glued to its midair position.

**Simple isolation 1.
Holding the ball.**

**Move the hand around
the ball.**

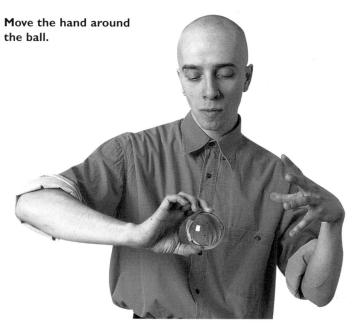

Ball above the hand.

Ball below the hand.

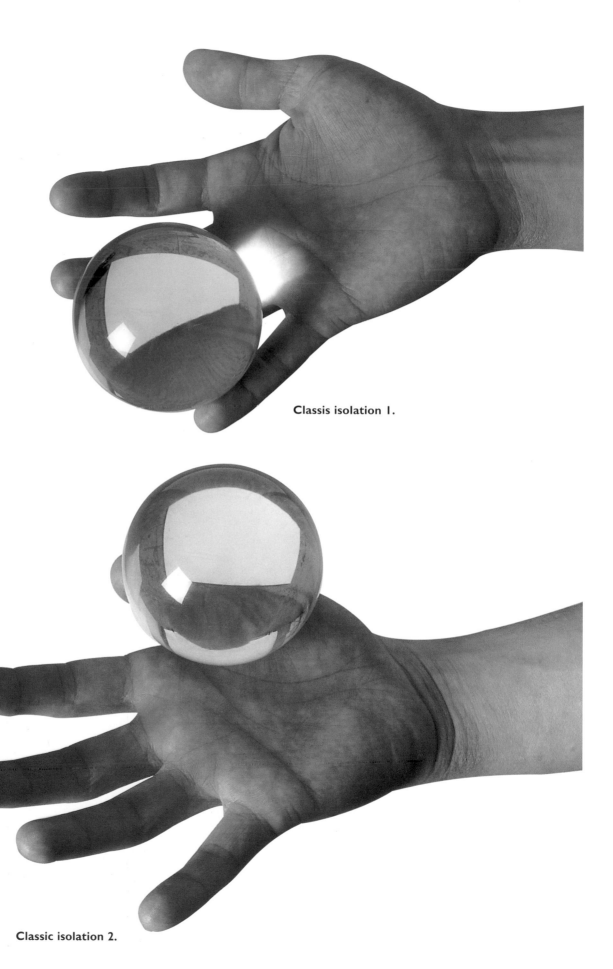

The classic isolation is a move that you can't practice enough. Place a ball in your right palm and try to encourage it to roll clockwise in a very small circle, supporting it with your fingers. Now try to get the ball to roll in increasingly large circles until it nearly rolls over your fingertips and the heel of your palm. (At first, you'll probably find that the path followed by the ball looks more triangular than circular—practice is the key to correcting this.) Now comes the hard part: start moving your hand beneath the ball while at the same time encouraging the ball to become still (focusing on a point behind the ball should again help).

92

Classis isolation 1.

Classic isolation 2.

**The correct line of vision:
focus on a spot behind the ball
and align the ball with it.**

Step 1.

Step 2.

When you've mastered the basic isolations, try changing hands while keeping the ball still. Your left hand should sweep in from the side, making counterclockwise, circular movements to get the motion going. Then change hands again.

While practicing changing hands, you could also try this easier, but still impressive-looking, move: slowly close your hand to form a fist, balance the ball on top (**1**), bring your other hand sweeping in from the side (**2**), and repeat the manouver (**3**). As before, your hands should be moving while the ball remains still.

94

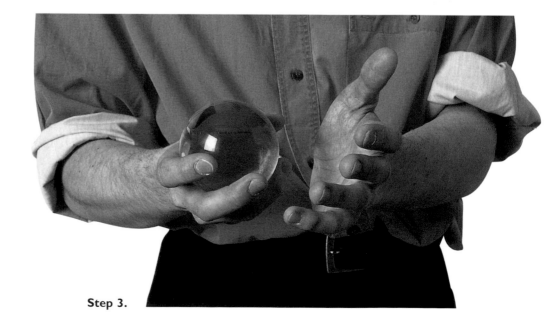

Step 3.

Palm-spinning

Spinning two or more balls in your palm so that they orbit each other is another way of contact-juggling. Although palm-spinning with two balls doesn't need any explanation, I can give you a few useful tips: firstly, small balls are usually easier for palm-spinning than larger ones; secondly, clockwise seems to be the easiest direction for the right hand to move in and counterclockwise for the left; and, thirdly, keep the balls separate and do not let them touch one another. Palm-spinning is closely related to isolations, so when you are palm-spinning two or more balls, try to keep one ball still, letting the others revolve around it.

Palm-spinning with three balls is easiest if the balls are hard and glossy, like pool balls. Place three in your strongest hand and let your thumb do most of the work. The hardest, but also the most important, requirement is that you relax: if your palm is tense, the balls will go nowhere.

When you've mastered palm-spinning with three balls, you'll find adding a fourth ball easy: simply place it on top of the three spinning balls. Keeping the stack of balls together requires a combination of relaxation and tension, and if it feels as though the stack is about to collapse, you're too relaxed.

Palm-spinning two balls.

Palm-spinning four balls.

95

Palm-spinning three balls.

Four-ball palm-spinning—the top ball is new.

Juggling
Practice

Juggling Practice

How much practice you will need to become a great juggler is a question that only you can answer. Some amateurs hardly practice at all, while professional performers may put in as many as twelve hours a day. Practice whenever you can, however, and you'll soon see the results. One advantage of juggling is that you can practice it more or less anywhere, so always try to carry a couple of balls around in your bag to take advantage of a spare moment in which to practice the latest trick that you've been struggling with.

Y ou will probably already have noticed that practicing with your weakest hand is boring, frustrating, and unrewarding. My theory is that this is because the brain is lazy: it's perfectly happy with the way things are and doesn't want to learn anything new, so when you're having difficulty with a juggling pattern, it's your brain's way of telling you to stop and do something that you already know instead. Once it has learned a new skill, however, your brain will be more cooperative, so resist the temptation to give up.

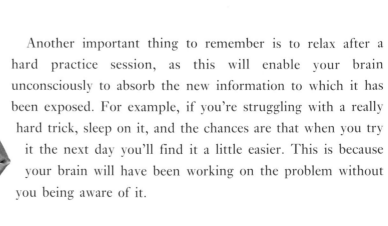

Another important thing to remember is to relax after a hard practice session, as this will enable your brain unconsciously to absorb the new information to which it has been exposed. For example, if you're struggling with a really hard trick, sleep on it, and the chances are that when you try it the next day you'll find it a little easier. This is because your brain will have been working on the problem without you being aware of it.

Try to change the way you practice every now and then. Lead with your weakest hand instead of your strongest when launching into a new pattern, for example, especially when you're practicing with four or five balls. It's not a good idea to do the same thing over and over again, as you'll easily fall into bad habits, and bad habits are hard to break.

Mastering the Impossible

If you're finding a pattern impossible to master, ask yourself whether you've really thought through what you're trying to achieve. Very complex patterns can be difficult to follow even before you add the balls to the equation. Play a slow-motion movie of what you're trying to do in your mind to help you to visualize which ball goes where before practicing the pattern for real. Alternatively, if you ask another juggler to juggle the balls slowly in front of you, the picture may become a little clearer.

Don't be afraid to attempt the impossible. If you're learning to juggle five balls, for example, try a couple of runs with seven balls; when you try the five-ball pattern again, it will seem much

easier. Constantly keeping yourself on edge in this way will help you to reach your targets more quickly.

When practicing passing patterns, especially multijuggler patterns in which you have to work out exactly where everything should go in advance, you may find floor-juggling helpful. Each of you should take a couple of balls before sitting on the floor and simply rolling them to one another. Because the passing is much slower, you have more time to analyze the pattern's movements.

Practice is, of course, the key when putting together a whole routine, be it a three-ball, contact-juggling, or passing routine, but proper planning is equally important. Write down all of the tricks that you know on Post-it (®) notes, stick them to a large board, move them around, and then discard the ones you're not happy with (and don't include ones that you can't perform five times in a row), keeping the ones that you like. Arrange the tricks so that the routine builds up to a finale, and don't forget to include lots of pauses. Members of your audience need to be given a pause every so often so that they can take in what they're watching—watching a juggler juggle an uninterrupted routine is rather like listening to someone talking without taking a breath.

Finally, spend time with other jugglers. Practice with them, ask them questions, and swap ideas with them. Most jugglers are sociable creatures who'll be pleased to demonstrate their skills to you. Also, try to go to juggling conventions, where you'll meet lots of fellow jugglers, play juggling games, and watch interesting shows.

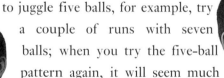

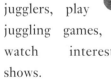

Notations

Notations

Over the years, jugglers have tried to devise ways of capturing juggling on paper, rather like musical notation. The trouble is, because juggling is so complex, there is no way of recording all of its aspects, such as hand positions, body throws, the number of balls used, the height of the throws, the type of spin, and so on. There are, however, two systems of notation that record some of these aspects: site-swap and ladder notation

Site-swap Notation

The commonly used site-swap notation uses numbers to represent throws, 3, for example, signifying the throw used in the three-ball cascade, 4 the throw used in the four-ball fountain, and so on. To put it simply, the numbers represent the height of the throw. If you were recording a five-ball cascade, for instance, you could translate it into a long string of 5s—5555555—every 5 representing a high crossing throw. Even numbers signify self-throws and uneven numbers crosses. A feed, in which a ball is placed in a receiving hand, is represented by a 1, while a 2 usually denotes a holding through the gap, as if one hand was going into two in one hand in a three-ball pattern and the other hand was simply holding the ball. A 0 signifies an empty hand, making the pattern 40 a two in one hand.

When writing site swap, we usually record only one sequence of the pattern, so that instead of writing 531531531, we simply write 531. When reading site-swap notation, the first thing to do is to work out the average of the numbers in the pattern to find out how many balls you will need. The average of 5, 3, and 1 is 3, making it a three-ball pattern. Start off by throwing a high crossing 5, the same throw that you would use in a three-ball shower or a five-ball cascade. The next throw is a 3 from the other hand, a crossing throw of the kind used in the three-ball cascade. When this ball peaks, feed the last ball, the 1, from the hand that threw the 5 into the other hand and then repeat the sequence. For practice, try reading, and then juggling, the patterns in the box above.

441: lead with a self-throw from each hand, then make a feed and repeat from the other side.

51: a simple shower.

55500: a three-ball flash, i.e., the three first throws of the five-ball cascade and then two gaps.

5551: a four-ball pattern, i.e., three consecutive fives followed by a feed.

53: a four-ball pattern, a lopsided cascade in which one hand throws fives and the other threes (called triple singles by club-jugglers, i.e., triples from one hand and singles from the other).

Site swap is useful when it comes to inventing new tricks, but it doesn't tell us from which side of the body the ball is thrown nor does it record simultaneous throws (although some jugglers claim that it does, the notation becomes very messy and hard to read). Furthermore, you can't tell if a throw goes under the leg or not, so it is useless for transcribing really flamboyant routines.

Ladder Notation

Ladder notation is a more visual way of capturing juggling on paper. Whereas site swap only describes the value of the throws, ladder notation captures the flight paths as well. Because each ball is drawn in a diagram, not only does ladder notation give the value of the throws, but a clear distinction between the right and left hand, too. It's also possible to record some body throws, like behind the back, as well as multiplexes and simultaneous throws.

The diagram, which is drawn from top to bottom, resembles a ladder, every step of the ladder representing one beat (as in site swap). By following the line, you can follow each ball through the pattern. Catches are represented by black (or full) circles and throws by white (or empty) circles. You can easily work out how many balls a pattern contains by counting the number of full circles (denoting full hands) at the top of the ladder.

If you look at a simple pattern like the three-ball cascade in ladder notation, some things will become clear about the pattern. For example, there's one throw every beat and also one catch every beat (when one hand throws, the other hand catches). It takes six beats for a ball to make a full circle of the pattern, while a throw and a catch take three beats, one of the beats being a hold and the other two beats being time spent in the air.

To clarify a pattern further, you could also enter the equivalent site-swap number beside a circle denoting a ball. When recording a pattern like Mills mess, in which you're crossing and uncrossing your hands, jotting down an "L" (for left) or a "R" (for right) on the side of the pattern could furthermore help you to understand which hand is responsible for which throw.

The ladders illustrated here represent different juggling patterns. The first is a simple three-ball cascade; the second is a three-ball cascade that incorporates a few tricks; the third is a Mills mess; and, finally, the fourth is the site-swap pattern 531. Look at them carefully, and you'll see that they make sense.

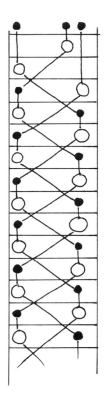

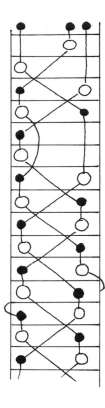

1 Simple three-ball cascade.

2 Complex three-ball cascade.

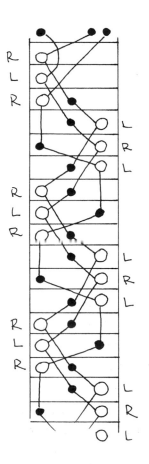

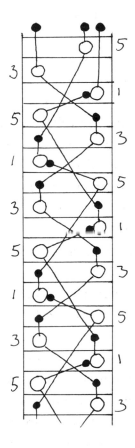

3 Mills mess.

4 Site-swap patttern 531.

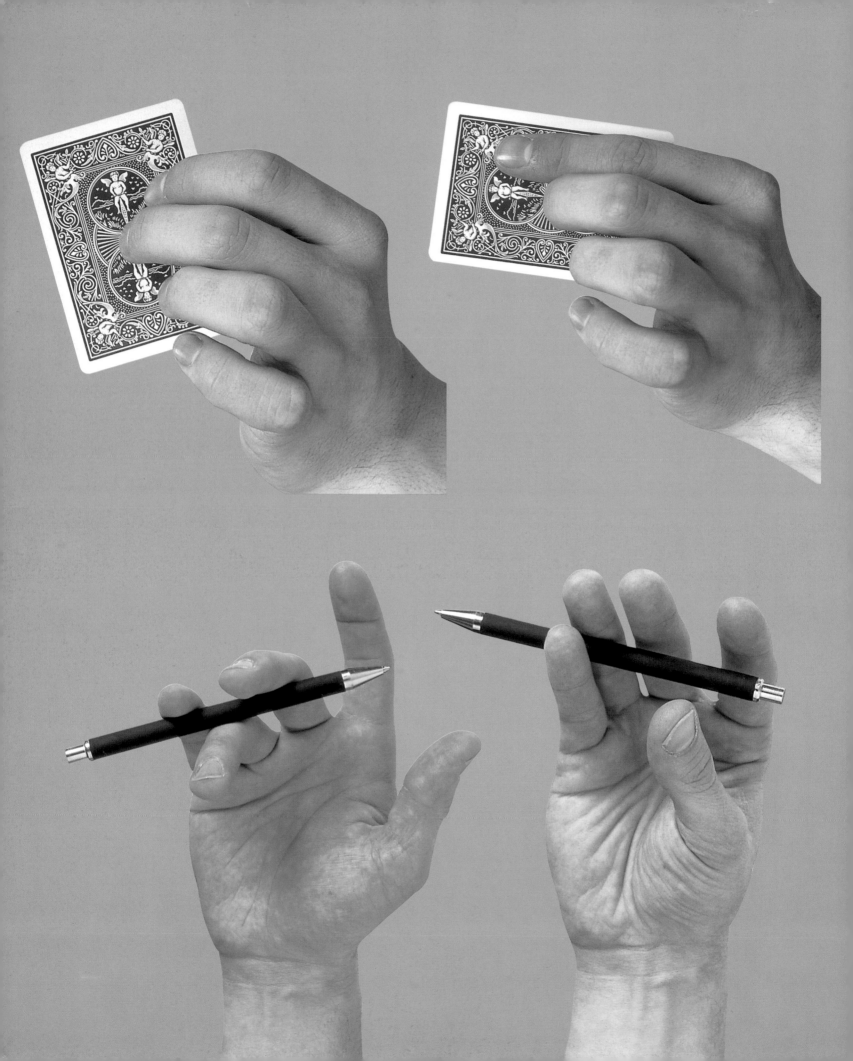

Miscellaneous Tricks

Miscellaneous Tricks

Although not strictly juggling, the following tricks, which some people would call party tricks or sleight of hand, will both keep your hands busy and impress your friends.

Pen Manipulation

Manipulating a pen between your fingers is something that you can practice wherever you are. In addition, embellishing a simple task with a thumb twirl gives it a certain flare.

In the thumb twirl, the pen makes a quick, unsupported turn around your thumb before you catch it in the usual writing grip. Hold the pen between your middle finger, your index finger, and your thumb (1). Your fingers should form a triangle on the upper part of the pen, with your thumb on the

opposite side. Now try to give the pen a little flick with your middle finger (2), so that the pen spins around your thumb (3) before you grip it in a comfortable writing position (4).

From this position, try a follow-up move. Place your ring finger on the opposite side of your middle finger and relax your thumb and index finger (5). Keep turning the pen counterclockwise (if you're working with your right hand). Place your little finger on the opposite side of your ring finger and then relax your middle finger (6). Swing the pen back up to its original starting position (7).

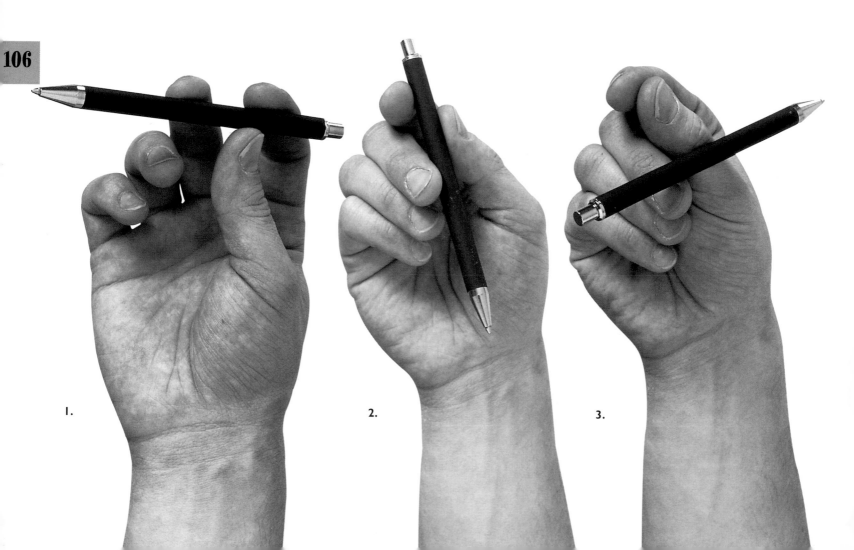

1.

2.

3.

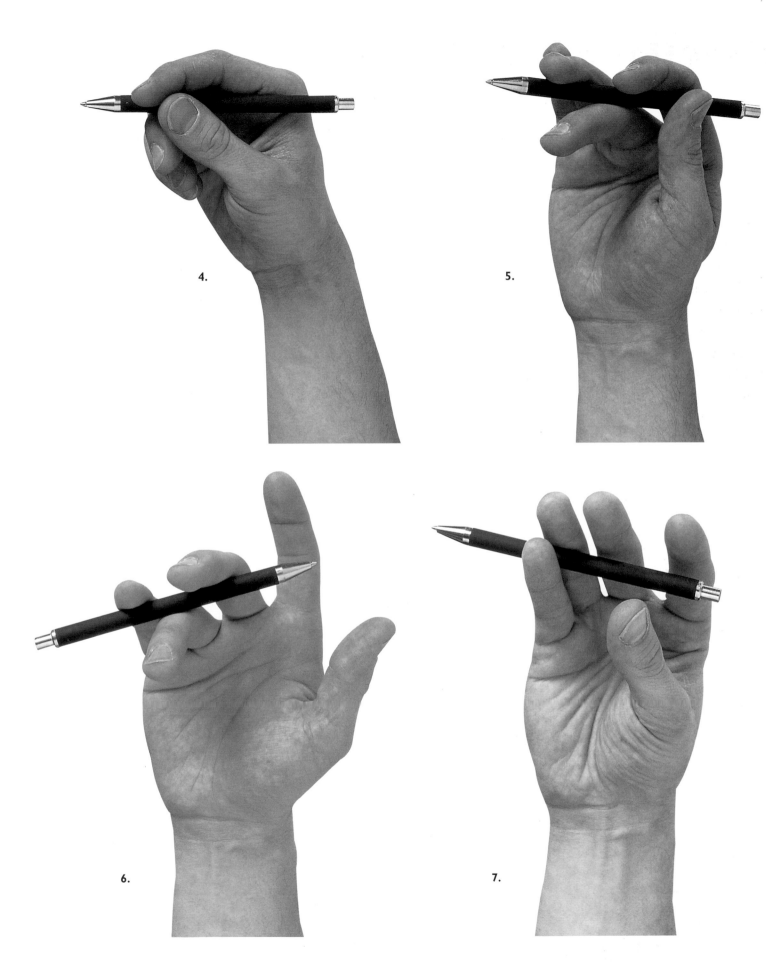

The Credit-card Spin

Another flashy move is the credit-card spin. Practice with an ordinary playing card at first. With your palm facing upward, and using your middle finger, find the center of the card and balance it for a while (1). Now place your thumb on the other side of the card and pinch the card between your thumb and middle finger (2). Place your index finger next to your middle finger and give the card a clockwise spin, at the same time releasing your thumb and index finger and letting the card spin on your middle finger for a while (3). The hardest part is building up the speed, and here your secret weapon is your index finger, which does so before letting go (4).

Once you've acquired the knack of this trick, use a credit card. (You'll find it easier if you hold it face down.) Because it's heavier than a playing card, you'll probably have difficulty spinning it more than twice. Two spins are nevertheless impressive.

I (seen from below).

2 (seen from below).

3 (seen from below).

4 (seen from above).

Index

A

ambidextrous 68

B

ball tricks 21–25, 28–37, 39–49
box 49
claw 42
columns 25
contortionist 43
elevator 32, 33, 40
juggling a gap 33
machine 40–41
Mills mess 44–47, 103
multiplex 34–35
one up, two up 29, 30–31, 43
over the head 48
over-the-top 22, 28
penguin 44
reverse cascade 28
rolling in 25
rolling out 25
split multiplex 34
splitting the brain 32
stacked multiplex 34, 36–37
three-ball cascade 7, 15–26, 28, 33,
44–47, 48, 103
two in one hand 24
under-the-hand 23
windmill 28

yo-yo 43 – *see also* patterns
balls 10–11, 13, 80, 81
acrylic 10, 91
color 10
silicone, 10, 11
see also props
beanbags 10, 12, 13, 61, 81
Brunn, Paul, 6

C

card tricks 108
cascade 7, 15–26, 28, 33, 34, 43, 44, 54,
61, 62, 63, 66, 103
catching 40–43, 70
Cinquevalli, Paul, 6
club-juggling 59–64
double spin 63
single spin 60–61
three-club cascade 62, 63, 67
club-passing 65–78
"every other" 66, 67
four count 66–67, 68, 73
one count 70
three around 67, 75
three count 68
two count 69
ultimates 70
club routines 71–72
"3–3–10" 71, 77
"4–4–8" 71, 72
box 77
running feed 77
club syncopations, 73
early double 73
late double 74
club tricks 63
double spin 63
high double 63

fish 75
Robin Hood 76
pincer 76
tomahawk 75, 76
under the leg pass 75
clubs 10, 11, 13, 62–66, 70
buying 11
grip 62 – *see also* props
contact-juggling 7, 11, 79–95
butterfly movement 82–83, 85
cradle grip 82, 85
isolation movements 89, 90–94
palm-spinning 95
transitions 84–90

Credits and Acknowledgments

The author and publisher would like to thank Karl Berseus for his skill and assistance during the photo shoot. Many thanks also to jugglers the world over, for their inspiration over the years.